EMBRACING THE CALM IN THE CHAOS

HOW TO FIND SUCCESS IN BUSINESS
AND LIFE THROUGH PERSEVERANCE,
CONNECTION, AND COLLABORATION

STACY IGEL

WITH EMILY LIEBERT

HarperCollins
Leadership

An Imprint of HarperCollins

For Dylan and Brian
I love you x Infinity x Infinity and beyond.
And to all of you who take risks!

Published by HarperCollins Leadership

Book design by Fritz Metsch

Any internet addresses, phone numbers, or company or product information printed in this book are offered as a resource and are not intended in any way to be or to imply an endorsement by HarperCollins, nor does HarperCollins vouch for the existence, content, or services of these sites, phone numbers, companies, or products beyond the life of this book.

ISBN 978-1-400-23493-6

e-ISBN 978-1-400-23509-4

Library of Congress Cataloguing-in-Publication Data

Library of Congress Control Number: 2022948337

———————————————

Printed in the United States of America

23 24 25 26 27 LSB 6 5 4 3 2 1

CONTENTS

ACKNOWLEDGMENTS

There are so many people I want to thank and not nearly enough space!

HUGE thank you to my literary agent, Kirsten Neuhaus, for believing in me every step of the way.

To my ghostwriter, Emily Liebert, I will never forget our first meeting and then the email seven years later. It was meant to be! Thank you for bringing this book to life with me.

To the amazing HarperCollins Leadership team: Sara Kendrick, Linda Alila, Sicily Axton, and Josh DeLacy. To Neuwirth & Associates for their immaculate production work.

To every single one of you who said yes to being in my book. All of you make me whole.

To all my childhood friends and college roommates for letting me dress you and photograph you. Without your love, I wouldn't have gotten this far.

To my BOY MEETS GIRL® team, partners, DJs, and licensing partners over the past twenty-plus years: we made—are making—incredible moments and milestones together. Those who have moved on: I love watching you grow in your subsequent roles, making a change in the world.

To my global warehousing, sourcing, and production partners: you are always cheering for me, and that is something I hold tight to the vest.

To Cliff: you and your team were crucial in helping me navigate mask production, warehousing, and shipping during a global pandemic.

To Guido: your vision is why our partnerships are successful and thriving.

To Ramit, Krupali, and the entire Tribal team for being incredible partners in our growing brands. I am thrilled for our next adventures.

To Jonna, for learning and growing with me and for bringing a positive attitude to work every single day.

To Munir, for being a partner and friend who has challenged me to become a stronger businesswoman. May we continue to soar and teach each other on this journey.

To Da and Nammie, for helping me while I was juggling both running a business and working on this book. I am forever grateful to both of you.

To my Dodi: you coined the words "keep moving" and believed in me, no matter what. Your love and wisdom kept me moving in dark times. I will love you to the end of time.

To Kathy: I am not sure where I would be without you. You are Wonder Woman and I am always inspired by you!

To Morgan, Sam, Max, and Bill: thank you for letting me dress you and pick your brains, even as you got older and I stayed the same age. I love being your aunt.

To Ronnie, George, Johanna, Matt, and Finn: thank you for your excitement and support always.

To my cousins around the world: you rock.

To my fierce grandmothers and aunts who inspired and believed in me: RIP.

To David Grann, who lent me his ear and time.

To Brian: thank you for building and creating a life with me. I could not be here without you and love you so very much.

To Dylan: thank you for inspiring me and making me a proud mama every single day.

And to my readers, for purchasing my first book and being part of my story. We did it! Now go out there and make things happen.

The road to achieving success is a long one—sometimes it's bumpy, sometimes it's smooth, sometimes it's absolute chaos. In my experience as a fashion designer and the founder of BOY MEETS GIRL®, a mission-driven, global, athleisure lifestyle brand, the best way to realize your goals is to embrace the calm in that chaos and *keep moving*.

Twenty-five years ago, while I was studying abroad in London, working for the iconic British designer Dame Zandra Rhodes, I heard the only joke from a friend that's ever stuck with me and, ultimately, defined my outlook on life, both professionally and personally.

There was a man who lived on the beach. First thing every morning, he'd take a long walk with his coffee and his newspaper. One day, as this man embarked on his walk, he wasn't in a good mood and noticed, much to his irritation, that there was a snail poking at his foot. Exasperated, he picked up the snail and threw it as far as he could. Ten years later, the man set out for his same walk with his coffee in hand. He opened his front door, bent down to pick up his newspaper, and there was the snail, who said, "Hey, man, what did you do that for?"

When I thought about why this joke resonated with me, I realized that it's because it's the perfect parable for building a company, which was my dream from a very young age. Of course I didn't understand what it would take to achieve that dream until I lived through it, but now that I'm on the other side, I've learned more than I ever could have expected.

The first thing I'll tell you is that entrepreneurship isn't easy, but it is rewarding. Along the way, you're going to have major successes. You're going to have failures and be let down. You're going to rise up and transcend. You're going to have disagreements. You're going to hire and fire employees, whether you like it or not. You're going to land a major deal, and maybe that deal will go sour, but then you'll get another deal, and everything will be great. The life of the snail is about the journey being the destination and about progressing at your own pace. It's about never giving up and pushing yourself forward—that's how I remain calm amidst the chaos.

What I always say to people starting out in fashion, or any industry, is that the clock doesn't stop, but you don't have to race against it. You do, however, have to work hard all the time and really believe in what you're putting out there. If you don't believe in what you're putting out there, and you can't differentiate yourself in the marketplace, don't bother. You have to think about what you want to do, who and where you want to be, and how you're going to get there. Things didn't always materialize immediately for me, but I had this excited and positive energy that kept me going.

Whatever you decide to be, whatever age you are, whether you're just starting out or you've taken a few laps around the block, you have to put in the hours and the elbow grease.

My story is about how I've grown my brand for twenty years, while handling challenges, doing what I love, and still being able to contribute to the world around me. Throughout my journey, as I learned the many lessons I'll impart in this book, I also relied on the wisdom of my friends and colleagues—those with whom I have an authentic connection and those who've supported me, discovered me, collaborated with me, built something that inspires me, made me laugh, and ultimately possessed the same level of passion that I do. I'll share some of their expert advice as well, as I'm a firm believer that gleaning knowledge from like-minded individuals is essential to progress.

As my friend Amy Serino, senior vice president of brand merchandising for the Atlanta Hawks and State Farm Arena, pointed out: "It's important to find your tribe early. You'll need these people several times throughout your career. The shared experiences and transparent point of view will be invaluable."

Becoming and being an entrepreneur is a wild ride. As I said, it will be chaotic at times, with or without your support network. My goal is to show you how I found peace within the madness and never stopped persevering, so that you can too.

EMBRACING THE CALM IN THE CHAOS

1

DON'T BE AFRAID TO EVOLVE

*Learn everything you can about your industry—
the world changes, so evolution should be a part
of your ongoing journey.*

In 2001, I launched my brand, BOY MEETS GIRL®. I was only twenty-four years old, which by most accounts is pretty young. Over the next twenty years, both my company and I evolved in ways and for reasons that I couldn't have imagined. But, before any of that happened, I wrote these exact words in my journal: *Success is measured by how much you want it.*

At the time, I had no idea how powerful that concept would become over the next two decades and throughout the trajectory of my career. The spirit behind that journal entry is part of the fabric of who I am, because I believe that part of wanting success is allowing yourself to evolve by not limiting your opportunities and experiences.

From a very early age, ambition was ingrained in me. One of the essential lessons of my family was that you can reach the top if you work hard enough. Even if you're not the best at something, you can still achieve your target, and the work you put in is what you'll see in the results.

As a result of this, my fascination with fashion design began to burgeon when I was only three years old. (I may have been yelling at my mom from the womb to let me plan a runway show!) Seriously, though, once I was old enough, I remember telling my mother precisely what I wanted to wear each day, whether it was dresses, sweatpants, or hoodies. It was part of my internal makeup.

My mom is a big thrift store shopper, so we used to go "thrifting" all around Bucktown and other areas of Chicago where I grew up. Through those experiences, I learned a lot about iconic designers, everyone from Chanel and Missoni to Donna Karan and Norma Kamali. I was very influenced, specifically, by the great women designers, leaders, industry standouts, and entrepreneurs, especially because my mom was a working mother, and I got to see her dressed in some of the pieces they created and wore, which sparked my passion for clothing and design.

My holy trinity of style goddesses begins with Coco Chanel, who famously said, "Fashion is not something that exists in dresses only. Fashion is in the sky, in the street, fashion has to do with ideas, the way we live, what is happening." I couldn't agree more with this statement. I love seeing style when I'm walking the streets in New York City and on the subway. I love it when I'm traveling anywhere in the world. Experiencing the motion of life inspires my creativity, my dedication to my craft, my collaborations, and my desire to raise awareness for many different causes. For me, it's about bringing a community together, which is why I'm so happy working as hard as I do.

Kate Moss is another beautiful and confident woman I've always admired. What I appreciate most about her is the way she effortlessly transitions from eclectic vintage to high fashion. She never looks like she's trying to put an outfit together—everything appears to naturally belong on her body. Last but definitely not least is singer-songwriter Patti Smith. She's remained true to her edgy chicness since the seventies and is an unflappable force of nature.

By the time I was seven, I was selling things like bracelets and charm necklaces to my classmates out of catalogs I assembled with

Polaroids of all the items. I had access to these pieces because my mom was both an entrepreneur and a physician assistant. She created a lumbar support called "The Back Machine," which was manufactured in Taiwan. She would travel there for work and come back with these accessories and other trinkets, like erasers and canteens, that were also being made in the same factory. What's crazy is that I still have those erasers and canteens and even a little bag with all my charm necklaces in it.

My mom was a ball of energy and a definite source of inspiration for me. I watched her run a business, fly overseas to inspect her products, and compete in marathons and triathlons while managing a household and taking my sister and me to 6:00 a.m. swim classes. This helped me understand what it means to be a woman entrepreneur and a working mom. She wasn't always the one who dropped me off or picked me up at school, but she tried to do as much as she could, and she did it with grace and without breaking down—I must have inherited my calm nature from her.

I also shadowed my mom at trade shows where she sold her Back Machine. Her industry was different from the fashion world in that she had only one style number, one colorway, one size, and one price point, which made for a very simple model. (If only I could keep my business that simple.) But at those trade shows, I studied the etiquette of how to operate a booth and sell to the customer who's buying your product.

Another thing I learned from my mom and my dad was the importance of giving back. My sister and I had *tzedakah* boxes (derived from the Hebrew root *tzedek*, meaning *justice*), and we were taught that donating resources to those in need is an act of integrity. We would put money into our boxes and, once it had accumulated, we'd pick nonprofits we were interested in. A portion of the sales from the knickknacks my mom brought home for me I contributed to organizations supporting anti-cruelty for animals and saving the environment.

I quickly realized that the more I sold, the more impact I could have on the world, which was another reason I wanted to develop that skill and continue to explore as much as I could about business. I started with little things, like lemonade stands with my sister outside our home in Chicago. This taught me the art of communicating with customers and also how to close a sale.

By the time I was eleven, my interests in selling and business took a clear turn toward fashion, compelling me to visit fabric stores in Chicago so I could make my own clothing. It was also at this time that I switched to a new school and, for my first day of sixth grade, I made my very first skirt with the help of my mother. It was a bold move considering I didn't know anyone and because the skirt was made from a houndstooth fabric that I'd hand sewn to match the pattern I'd purchased along with it. It had an elastic waist, and everything was super jagged.

My mom looked at the finished product and said to me, "Take pride in the work you put into it, and believe in yourself," which instilled in me a level of confidence that's so important for young women. Believing in yourself and what you do is half the battle. Even if I got judgmental looks from other girls, which I know I did, I didn't care. My feeling was, *I made this skirt, and I'm owning it!* It was this gumption that led me to make friends who would come over to my house, where I'd "produce" runway shows by styling them in my clothing or pieces I'd created.

While I loved putting on those "events" at home, my ambition for styling, selling, and exposing myself to the fashion industry continued to push me. As a result, I applied for and landed my first real retail job as a salesperson at the Gap when I was only twelve years old, which was no easy task. I interviewed with three different managers and one senior manager. I explained that even though my only prior work experience had been lemonade stands and helping my mother with her business, I lived and breathed fashion and had a knack for folding clothing and styling my friends.

Since bodysuits were a trend at the time, I also impressed them with my awareness of French designer André Courrèges, who'd created one of the first bodysuits in the mid-1960s as a symbol of women's liberation.

That job at the Gap was crucial in nurturing my business, retail, and fashion skills—I still have the pin I wore when I worked there. (I'm a sentimentalist, or maybe a pack rat; it's a fine line.) It encouraged me to continue sketching and creating my own clothing, as I was surrounded by apparel that spoke to the masses, and I wanted to do the same thing in my own way. Additionally, it helped me learn the ins and outs of merchandising, what it was like to work for a major chain, and how it felt to make my own money and know that I could buy my own bodysuits.

The experience wasn't without its challenges. Since I was so young, I was super scared the other employees would look down on me. I did make a handful of mistakes at checkout, but everyone was very patient, and that patience was a helpful lesson in how to be a manager.

After a month of working there, I'll never forget walking into the cramped lunch-break room, where sales goals and acknowledgments were posted each week. I looked up at the wall and didn't see my name right away, which upset me since I'd thought I was doing so well. As my eyes traveled higher, I noticed it instantly. It said that I was the "top dog" seller of the week. I couldn't believe that I'd outperformed all the adult salespeople. It felt like someone was publicly patting me on the back, which was so gratifying.

I wrote in my journal many years later:

There it was: TOP DOG OF THE WEEK. Stacy Morgen-stern. My heart dropped. It was the summer of 1989, and I was the top dog seller at the Gap in my home town Chicago. . . . I don't remember a time in my life when I wasn't into fashion and the beat of it. I think that top dog week is something I clearly have never forgotten. It gave me the fuel to keep doing what I love, and I guess that summer it was in retail selling.

For that reason, I've always been self-motivated and have never felt pressure from my parents or anyone else. I just put pressure on myself to be the best I can be. And that's a very lucky situation to be in. No one ever said I needed to be a banker, a lawyer, or a doctor. I had a lot of creative freedom in my pursuits, but it was made clear to me that if I wanted to maintain that freedom, I had to learn all facets of whatever business I pursued. There were no free rides.

When I got to high school, unfortunately they didn't offer any classes in fashion or design. I had to forge my own path, a constant theme throughout my life. There was never a box I fit in. I created it, because I realized there was no straight line to success.

To do that, I interned at the local Merchandise Mart and shadowed one of the other employees so I could learn what a sales representative did. I also worked at a store called Fox's in Chicago before eighth grade (Fox's is an off-price seller of high fashion labels, also located in New York City). In the summer before my junior year of high school, I took a class at Chicago's Columbia College on sketching and design. I would go to various stores, find old fabrics, and outline future collections.

I created my own high school prom dress, as I'd done a whole study on the Roaring Twenties. It was a flapper-inspired dress with a silk fringe trim, and it was my first piece of clothing where I made the pattern on my own. I had someone help me sew it because I still didn't have my own sewing machine and had never worked with woven fabric (which is non-stretch fabric). It's cool to see all the sewing machines and sewing classes that young girls have access to these days; I wish I had that back then.

As a means of expanding my horizons even further, I took photography classes during my senior year of high school so I could hone my eye and allow myself to develop in all areas connected to my pursuit. And I had a job outside of school at Marshall Field's department store. For the interview, I had to stand in front of thirty people and demonstrate how I would sell a wallet to a customer. I guess I was convincing enough, because they assigned me to the hosiery department, which, for me, was very interesting since I was determined to learn and absorb as much knowledge as I could to become a future fashion mogul. Very early on, I recognized that my evolution would continue by piecing together all these prospects for myself.

Once I was in college at the University of Wisconsin-Madison, I continued to carve out my own journey and forge my own path. I triple majored in retail, design, and business. I crafted a program for myself with the head of the design school, which allowed me to have a one-on-one experience my junior and senior years and create my own collection and thesis. This was not something other students were doing, but I knew how important it was for me to learn more about business and retail and not only design. Thus I earned a business certificate from the Wisconsin School of Business (at the University of Wisconsin-Madison) as well. Even though this was not the "normal" path for students, it worked for me and for them.

The summer of my sophomore year, I was itching to head to New York, where I got an internship at Donna Karan's company through a college friend who knew the person who ran the human resources department there. She sent in my résumé, and I was hired after a detailed phone interview. The only way I was able to afford to go that summer was because my sister, who's five years older than I am, already lived there, so I had a place to stay. I slept on her couch with her roommates also living in the apartment and, each day, I took the crowded subway to 40th Street in the heart of New York's Garment Center. Walking by all the fabric stores, passing all the people on the streets, and entering Donna Karan's building was my calm in the land of fashion chaos.

While at Donna Karan, I learned about trade shows, merchandising, working with buyers, and wholesale. Back then, Donna Karan had a line called the D collection. Even though Donna Karan's company was massive, for some reason I had a very intimate experience there, because I was able to focus on that smaller collection. I got to see how a designer comes up with a new concept and the factors that influence whether a concept will sink or swim.

In my junior year of college, I was accepted into a program abroad in London, where they focused on design, Fashion Week shows, and trend forecasting. I got an internship with Dame Zandra Rhodes, an iconic textile designer known for her use of bright colors. She's collaborated with brands ranging from Valentino to IKEA.

I worked in her pattern-making room, which was in her home, and got to see her styling and sketching. She was coming out with a home line, so I helped design and publicize it. I had the privilege of witnessing this legend do so much with a very lean, but mighty, team, and that gave me a lot of hope for my future.

After my work study abroad in London, I returned to New York for four weeks the following summer and found a dorm room at New York University with a roommate I didn't know. My mother went to hear Elsa Klensch speak in Chicago, with me in mind, and gave her my résumé, so I reached out to CNN because she had a show called *Style with Elsa Klensch*. She was the first woman to bring a fashion-focused program to TV, long before the advent of social media and influencers. Her show was the only source of dedicated fashion news, and I was intrigued by that. Elsa wasn't a designer but she was interviewing all the major industry leaders, and I desired a better understanding of the communication side of things. Ultimately, I was hired to do the internship because I was relentless—I called CNN about a hundred times until I got my now friend Jon Filmon on the phone. I told him: "This internship is for me. I will do *everything* for you and your team. Please hire me."

While I was interning for Elsa, I got to interview Marc Jacobs at his show downtown in the Bowery and ride in limousines around New York City with Elsa talking about her days at *Vogue*. It was wild but also very grassroots and hands on, and I soaked it up like a big sponge. I had to transcribe every interview, and I was quick at it (must have been those impromptu typewriting classes working with my mom on her business). I also went to fashion shows with Elsa at Bryant Park and became completely obsessed with the frenetic energy. I would see Bill Cunningham running around shooting street style for the *New York Times* in his blue jacket and watch Anna Wintour glide through the halls like she was on the catwalk. If there was one thing I knew, it was how much I loved the whole business and, in turn, this passion led me to work even harder, especially when things seemed overwhelming.

The thing is, some internships don't pay but may give class credits, which was the case for me, so during my senior year at Wisconsin I got a job as a salesperson at a local boutique called Scoshi. Thanks to my unfailing ambition, my boss gave me this chance, which was a real coup for me as a college student. While I was there, I was one of four organizers of an annual fashion show at Wisconsin, an all-day event through the apparel and textile design program. It was held at Tripp Commons in Memorial Union in Madison, and I assumed the role of multimedia coordinator. The show had constant music provided by six different spinners throughout the day, and there was a ten-foot video screen that showcased the models, who were a mix of professionals and students, as they walked down the runway. I also made a hundred sophisticated hippie sack tops, some of which were worn by the professional models. I sold the rest to Scoshi so they could carry my product, as well as to college friends who would act as mobile models for me. It was my first time seeing my product in a retail store. It was also my first time seeing customers react so positively to my product.

Model I cast for my University of Wisconsin fashion show, wearing my first top I designed in college

When spring break rolled around, a group of us landed on a sweet deal to go to Acapulco, and my friends wore my shirts while we were there. Everyone was asking where they bought them, which is how I got customers from so many different schools. There was no social media and there were no cell phones back then. When someone purchased my shirt, it wasn't like I could connect with that person again online.

I remember calling my mom from a pay phone in Acapulco on our last day of spring break and saying, "Mom, I only have two shirts left, and we're leaving!" I was so thrilled about sharing the news with her that I didn't notice this guy standing next to me.

He overheard my conversation and asked, "What are you selling?"

I told him I'd designed my first shirts and that they were modern-day, hippie-sack-inspired tops made of satin and metallic fabrics.

He said, "Why don't you come upstairs, and I'll buy the last two from you."

I'm not sure what possessed me to follow a complete stranger to his hotel room on spring break in Acapulco as my friends were waiting for me in the cab to head to the airport, but the mystery man turned out to be Noah Tepperberg, who was at that time a big party promoter in New York City and since then has cofounded several nightclubs and restaurants, including Marquee, TAO, Avenue, and LAVO.

When we got upstairs, Noah introduced me to his partner, Jason Strauss. He said: "This is Stacy, and she's selling her shirts. These are her last two, and we're going to buy them from her."

That's how I met Noah (he bought one of the shirts for his sister Judy), who became my friend and nightlife coordinator during those early years in New York City.

I got back into the cab with my friends, and everyone was so pumped. I was like: *Oh my God, I'm really doing this. I'm pursuing what I love!* Even then I knew that was the greatest gift of all. I also understood that real success wouldn't happen overnight, but if I continued to allow myself to evolve, I could keep moving and amazing things would happen.

✓ Working hard and learning many different facets of your chosen passion will allow you to grow and advance.

✓ Figure out who your influences are and recognize that they can change over time.

✓ Be relentless about charting your path and pursuing what you want. Perseverance is part of evolution.

✓ Ask yourself what kind of impact you'd like your business to have on the world. What kind of footprint do you want to leave behind?

2

BE UNSTOPPABLE

*If you believe that you're unstoppable, you'll own
the risks you take and keep moving, learning, and building.*

In order to keep my momentum going after graduating from
college in 1999, I knew I had to move to New York City, the
epicenter of the fashion world, and find a job in the industry.
Of course this is easier said than done, but I kept reminding myself
that I couldn't let anything stand in the way of my dream.

Fortunately, a few of my best friends from college also had their
eyes on Manhattan and my sister was still living there, so four of us
decided to share an apartment in order to afford the rent. After
looking at what felt like a thousand spaces that could accommodate
multiple people without breaking the bank—a feat in and of itself
in New York City—we eventually agreed on a two-bedroom that
we converted to a four-bedroom, which was practically a miracle.

My first job as a newly minted New Yorker was as an assistant
designer for the brand Elie Tahari. I had interviewed for a job with
a company called Delia's during Christmas break in my senior year
and got it. However, right as I was packing up to move to New York
City, a friend of my sister's said there was an opening at Tahari. I
was torn, as I'd worked so hard to get the job at Delia's by calling
the main number repeatedly until they gave me the direct line for

human resources. I had to really think about what my goals were, and I knew that the Tahari position was a better direction for me. I felt that through my experiences with Zandra Rhodes and Elsa Klensch, I'd had direct access to the person running the show, and I loved learning under those leaders. I knew Elie was also very hands-on at his company, and being able to learn from the creator or founder was something I wanted to continue.

When I found out that I got that job, too, I had to call Delia's two weeks before my start date to tell them I was sorry but I would not be joining their team. I remember it like it was yesterday. I was at a pay phone on 42nd Street watching the hustle of the city and the big screens in Times Square. My heart was beating hard against my chest, even though I was confident in my decision. Thankfully, they understood, as does my friend Tracey Smith, head of celebrity and influencer talent for LL Cool J's "Rock the Bells," who believes, "Confidence is knowing that taking leaps of faith will always work out in your favor."

While at Tahari, my responsibilities ranged from manning the front desk to sales and merchandising to buying trim in the Garment Center to helping design women's suits to acting as a fit model in Elie's showroom for his button-down shirts. It was the beginning of my career, so I was also getting coffee for people and answering the phones. Instinctually I wanted to create and offer my input on everything, but I understood that there was a time and place for that, so I just kept my head down and worked. No task was too big or too small. It was weekdays, weekends, and late nights, because we were a small group of people in an intimate setting, and I was insatiable in my quest for knowledge. Something I've always taught my employees is that you can't sit back and watch what's happening in front of you or wait for someone to call your name; you have to get in there, roll up your sleeves, and become part of the action. And that's exactly what I did, which definitely reinforced my passion.

My friend and colleague Veronica Webb, who is a supermodel, actress, and content writer, advises the same thing: "Keep your eye on the prize and identify what you're working toward. If you're just out there every day, like choose me, pick me, then you don't really have much to anchor yourself to. Many young women don't realize that they need concrete goals."

Sure, there are people working for fashion houses who leave at 6:00 p.m., but I recognized early on that if I wanted to have my own business one day, I had to get used to giving all of myself to my career, which was part of my intrinsic nature anyway. There would be opportunity later in life to find that personal-professional balance that everyone seeks, but at this point, I was twenty-two years old and hyper focused on the professional side of things.

One of my oldest friends from childhood Meredith Weintraub, an executive producer at the *Rachael Ray* show, offered this piece of advice to people starting out in any career: "Try to anticipate the needs of the person you report to. Once you do that, you can work to support them by completing tasks before being asked. By keeping in mind the million little things that need to get done and checking them off the list, you free your boss up to think about the big picture, instead of the minutiae of the day-to-day. It shows that you are an attentive go-getter who can handle your workload without the need for constant oversight, making you a vital team member. Plus, it demonstrates that you know the needs of the role above you—so when an opportunity to move up arises, it is clear that you are up to the task."

As I got my feet wet in the corporate arena, I was also creating my own pieces out of my apartment so I could continue the momentum I'd started in college. When I got home from work, I would sew in my bedroom late at night and into the early morning hours. Who needed sleep? My male cousins would give me their vintage Levi's jeans, and I would shop vintage menswear pants and turn them into bags. I did this by cutting up the legs of the jeans and pants and sewing the bottom of one open pattern while sewing the top of the other open pattern with a clean seam and then using the open side to insert the bag handles. I loved lining the denim with vintage menswear patterns. I also made vintage tops with ribbons and sold them to friends of friends. My roommates were, as usual, my walking billboards. They would go shopping in the East Village, SoHo, and NoHo, and the buyers at the stores would ask, "Where did you get that?" and "Where can I get that?" Or they'd go out with other friends who would want shirts like the ones they were wearing. It was all word of mouth, and what started happening was that we'd have friends of friends of friends who would come to our apartment and commission me to design one-of-a-kind pieces for them.

Another one-of-a-kind creation made in my home atelier

COURTESY OF STACY IGEL

One of the big challenges I faced, between my day job and the new responsibility of making my own clothing and accessories, was that there wasn't much time left for a social life. But I'm a social person, so I craved having one. When we did go out, I would stay up working even later that night, the next day, or work through the weekend to make up for it. These are the sacrifices you have to make to reach your goals.

Being an entrepreneur, at whatever stage you're in, is a somewhat selfish prospect. That selfishness doesn't originate from a negative place, it's just that you have to know what to focus on if you want to succeed, which for me was producing these one-of-a-kind pieces that I could sell to everyone and anyone who was asking.

Still, even with the hype surrounding my creations, I knew I wasn't ready to branch out entirely on my own just yet. I wanted to make sure that my skills were as varied as possible, since different companies and labels have their own unique ways of doing things. Then, to my complete astonishment, I was fired from Elie Tahari. One night, after office hours at 10:00 p.m., the president of the company saw my colleague putting lipstick on me for an event, and she let me go the next day.

I was not only shocked but so disheartened, especially since she offered no explanation. I didn't understand how someone with my unfailing work ethic, who'd devoted herself completely to this company, could be laid off for something so seemingly insignificant. I'd worked around the clock, did what was asked of me, and I'd never missed a day on the job. I know that many people get fired at least once in their life, but it was still completely horrifying for me.

I left there feeling numb and immediately called my best friend and roommate, Ami, and my sister to meet me on the Lower East Side so I could cry my eyes out. It was a dreary day in New York City. We walked past some of my favorite stores, and I remember buying a vintage purple coat for some retail therapy.

I quickly went from numb to angry. But I still had to pay my rent, and once I'd taken a little time to process everything, I told myself that I couldn't let one circumstance waylay me. To keep moving forward, I had to be unstoppable. I summoned my calm in that chaos by calling a recruiter I'd been introduced to via my friends at Tahari. I updated my résumé and design portfolio, met with him the next day, and then went on a dozen interviews to find my next step.

I ended up landing a new job at Izod, which was a complete one-eighty from life at Tahari—now I was involved with menswear, like golf shirts rather than women's suits, and not working directly with the founder, but my boss there had the same work ethic as the team at Tahari. She worked hard and stayed until 10:00 p.m., and I never left before she did. Once you've had more experience and climbed the ranks, it's okay if your boss works later than you do, as long as you've completed your responsibilities. But at this stage in a career, showing that you're putting in the hours really makes a difference, and that dedication is crucial to survival and longevity. At least it was for me.

While I was at Izod, just as I had at Tahari, I kept up with my own designs on the side. Over the Christmas holidays, I made mitten holders embroidered with strawberries, pears, and cherries—inspired by my childhood and because I'm a kid at heart. Many of my colleagues at Izod bought them for themselves and as gifts for their family members, which was such a fun intersection of both of my worlds.

One important thing I would tell anyone looking to be an entrepreneur is that you need to work for other brands or companies before launching your own venture. Experience is king. It makes you well rounded and helps you learn and engage in things that may not seem directly connected to your chosen interest. For example, you can't just know about fashion design if you want to run your own company. You have to learn the financial side of things and publicity and marketing. You also have to understand how to manage a staff—something I wish I'd done more of before going out on my own. In my earlier experiences at the Gap/Scoshi/Fox's, I was introduced to the areas of retail and merchandising. At Zandra Rhodes, I was exposed to publicity, design, and small business functions. At Donna Karan, sales and marketing; at Elsa Klensch, communications; and at Elie Tahari and Izod, design and sales.

I always knew, deep in my soul, that I was going to build something on my own—something much more extensive than creating one-of-a-kind items in my bedroom. I just didn't know exactly when it would happen. I figured I would continue to immerse myself in my work and, eventually, the timing would feel right.

Of course, life doesn't always follow a playbook. As I was busy remaining persistent on the career front, I met my now husband, Brian, at a bar in 2000. I definitely wasn't looking for a boyfriend. I was *not* someone who moved to New York to find a man, get married by a certain age, and have a baby a year later. Then, unexpectedly, I encountered this amazing person who challenged me and who was very different from anyone I'd dated in the past. I was a midwestern girl and he was a New Yorker, but he had a down-to-earth spirit that I loved. It became clear almost immediately that we were on the same page in life.

At the time, Brian was working in marketing at Chelsea Piers, a sports complex, and I was in the midst of hustling at my day job and sewing in my bedroom by night. The only reason I managed to fit in a relationship is because he valued my ambition and dedication to my craft and was there to hang out with me at midnight when I'd finished my work. Fortunately, Brian was excited about my future prospects. This brings me to another point: as an entrepreneur, you want to find people who are willing to build your dream with you.

I'm pretty sure I knew Brian was the one when he trekked around the Lower East Side with me on the weekends, selling my vintage bags and tees. He would wait outside on the corner while I took my rolling bag into each shop. I'll never forget a really awesome Vespa store that had no business selling handbags and shirts, but I convinced the owner to buy them on the spot and that it would be cool to hang them on his scooters. My sales tactic was that he was surrounded by both vintage and new clothing stores but he didn't sell any clothing himself. I told him that if his windows showcased hip, upcycled clothing and bags, he would sell more Vespas.

I should also point out that there were a lot of places that turned me away. When a buyer passes on something you've poured your heart and soul into, it sucks, but rejection is a big part of the game and you can't let it stunt your progress. Instead, use it as fuel to get what you want. I asked my longtime friend Jackie Tohn, actress, comic, host, musician, and show creator, if she faced rejection on her journey. She noted: "There's an almost inconceivable level of rejection that comes with choosing a high-profile career. Managing expectations and getting over heartbreak as quickly as possible are two important skills to cultivate. That might sound dark, but it's a necessity. Of course you can find unparalleled joy and wonder in the successes of any business, but it's a long haul, so prepare as best you can for the ups and downs. I always say, no matter what profession you're going into, there will be rejection. And understanding that is super important as you embark on the steps to building your career."

Once I'd made some rounds in New York City, I decided it would be smart to get a taste of retail in Los Angeles, and I also wanted to visit one of my best friends from childhood, Ike Barinholtz, who was an up-and-coming actor. Ike was close with Seth Meyers from his days at Boom Chicago, so the two of them took me to the Fred Segal store, which is a local institution that helped define the "California cool" aesthetic. Seth and Ike waited outside, like Brian had in New York City, while I went in with my rolling suitcase of vintage bags and shirts. (Unlike Brian, however, they waited in a car, because nobody walks in Los Angeles.) When I came back outside, I had a big smile on my face, and I announced, "I sold my designs to Fred Segal!" I had no idea how I was going to make all the product so I could be paid for it, but I told myself I'd figure it out when I got back to New York. That's what entrepreneurs do. They figure it out, no matter how steep the challenge is.

That night we all went out to celebrate, and Seth found out that he'd been offered the job as a writer on *Saturday Night Live*, which was so crazy. We were excited young kids doing our thing and working really, really hard to get by. I knew, then and there, that I was ready to branch out on my own.

Ike, who's now a well-known actor, writer, producer, and director, told me that he remembers that day well: "It made me realize that you have to put yourself out there and find what you really love. Then you have to think about it and work on it every day. If you're truly passionate about something, it will be all-consuming."

When I returned to New York, I went back to my job at Izod and asked the vice president, Helen Katz, if I could speak with her. I said, "You know, I'm making my own clothes by night and selling them, and I would love to work here four days a week, so I can focus on my business on the fifth day." It was a courageous move that could have been received very badly, but Helen was wonderful, and she knew how committed I was.

She said, "Let me think about that." The next day, she called me into her office and told me that she'd spoken with a bunch of people about my request. "We will offer you Fridays off at the same salary." Holy shit! I couldn't believe that she was going to effectively give me a raise, and I was so thankful. You should never be ashamed or fearful of asking for what you think is right and fair for yourself.

I started working four days a week at Izod, and I was sewing more and more by night, so much so that by the time Friday came around, it was hard for me to muster the same energy for my own venture, which wasn't what I had hoped for. I went back to Helen a month later and said: "Thank you so much for giving me the opportunity to work four days a week and have one day off, which is such a rare gift. I'm so grateful that you believed in me. But I can't possibly cram my own business into one day a week and weekends if I want it to take off. Sadly, I have to leave Izod and spread my wings."

I was leading with confidence and courage. As scary and tough as it was for me, I had to take this entrepreneurial leap. My friend Sabina Hitchen, the founder of Press for Success and a small business expert, discussed the topic of confidence with me: "You don't become a swimmer by reading about swimming, talking about swimming, and watching people swim. You dive into the water and do it."

As I see it, there are many professional paths you can pursue. In my case, I'd observed all these great leaders within their own organizations—from Donna Karan, Elsa Klensch, and Elie Tahari to Zandra Rhodes—and I just couldn't envision myself within one of those establishments anymore. I had to do my own thing, which I often say can be a curse, because it's a tremendous burden to bear when you sacrifice financial security to sew clothing in your bedroom. But creating and fashion design were my destiny, and I had to take that risk.

I remember calling my parents and explaining to them that I was quitting my well-paying, full-time job to start my own company. I told them that I would pick up some freelance work to make ends meet, but that I wouldn't have my 401(k) or my health benefits. I'm sure they knew how scared I was, but they never once discouraged me. They also made it abundantly clear that they were not going to pay my rent. They urged me to really weigh the pros and cons and challenged me with the hard truth—that there would be no financial fallback, no matter what happened.

Regardless, I took a leap of faith and went out on my own. If that's your ambition, I want to embolden you to do the same thing.

✓ Venturing out on your own is scary, but working with different brands and exploring other markets first will help allay your fear and empower you to be unstoppable.

✓ Don't let rejection get in your way. Stay calm and roll with the punches. Remember that rejection helps build character and endurance.

✓ Find people who will build your dream with you.

✓ You'll have to make sacrifices. Consider which ones you can live with.

3

DISTINGUISH
YOURSELF FROM THE PACK

*By distinguishing yourself from the pack, people will
notice you and progress will ensue.*

Hen I first started BOY MEETS GIRL®, I knew I wanted to create a message and a logo that spoke to everyone. One of the many ways I embrace the calm amid the chaos in my life and career is to constantly distinguish myself from those around me, because my style is different from everything else on the market. I had studied all the major brands and what made them resonate with consumers over time. I'd always been fascinated by the widespread appeal of Ralph Lauren's polo player and how Missoni's fabrics have a very specific and recognizable identity.

What I didn't expect was to find inspiration for my brand at my boyfriend Brian's house the first time I met his parents. I walked into their home and immediately noticed these silhouettes on the wall, which I was told were sketches of Brian, his sister, and his brother when they were children. I stood directly in front of Brian and his parents and said, "You're not going to believe this, but I have the exact same silhouettes of me and my sister." I knew it was a sign. I realized that those silhouettes were a reflection of the stages of our lives and could tell a visual story of someone's experiences, no matter who they were or where they came from—a first friend, a first kiss, or a first boyfriend or girlfriend. It was branding genius staring me in the face.

About a week later, I grabbed the silhouettes of me and my sister that I'd carried with me from Chicago to New York City when I moved. I took them to Brian's house, we scanned them into the computer, and tinkered with them in Photoshop. At first, it was individual silhouettes of me and Brian. Then I merged them together, we puffed up the hair a bit, and manipulated a few more design elements. Once we were done, I stepped back, examined the finished product, and said, "Boy Meets Girl." There was no question about it.

"Boy Meets Girl" just rolled off my tongue, so I trademarked the name and the logo Brian and I had created, and my brand became BOY MEETS GIRL®. Instinct told me that the logo would speak to the masses. It wasn't a love story—it was *everybody's* story.

With my new name and logo trademarked, I was ready to tackle my first trade show—the Workshop NY trade show—which featured sixty designers who'd been selected by submitting portfolios of their designs. Since I'd left my full-time job to build my own company, being accepted into this show was extremely important to me, which must be why I was sweating through my top as I explained the essence of my brand to the woman who ran it. At the same time, I was also confident in my capabilities and my open point of view. When she told me I'd made the cut, I knew it could change my career forever. I was among some fashion greats: Gary Graham, known for his attention to detail, craftsmanship, and the historical culture of women's clothing; and Peter Som, noted for his use of color, pattern, and effortless feminine silhouettes.

My first collection was definitely different from everyone else's. It included hoodies, sweatshirts and sweatpants, and T-shirts with my BOY MEETS GIRL® logo printed on them. I also had upcycled vintage T-shirts with sleeves that I'd embroidered and transformed as a nod to my thrifting days growing up and into my twenties. My pieces represented a reflection of the past as well as a look into the future. I had found fabric in the Garment Center that was vintage-inspired floral embroidery, and I was able to buy yards of it in different colors. Then I used the embroidered fabric to sew dramatic sleeves onto the fitted bodice of the T-shirts and made a little cinch at the center of the chest so it was ruched, creating a hippie-bohemian look.

COURTESY OF STACY IGEL

On top of those designs, I also fashioned what I called "Ribbon Cinch" shirts, which were like nothing I'd seen before and ended up being an important part of my collection. They had an eclectic feeling to them and were inspired by all these ribbon designs I'd found in the Garment Center. Initially, I sewed the shirts myself and made the same little cinch that fell right at the center between the breasts, which flattered every woman, no matter her shape or size. The cinch came two-and-a-quarter inches down the shirt from

HPS (high point shoulder), and it had to be exact. Eventually, I hired one sewer to help me make them, because I had developed a special and very specific "trade dress" pattern, and I didn't allow anyone else to touch them for a long time. Even back then, I was scared of being copied. I grouped my ribbons into different themes: solids, rainbow, stripes, dots, stars for Americana, and animals. And I implemented this "Ribbon Cinch" on different styles of short-sleeve, long-sleeve, and tank tops.

I knew that the Workshop NY trade show was a major opportunity to showcase these items and prove my talent to real buyers who could put me on the map if they liked what they saw. It's one thing to be unique and another to share that in a public forum. To move forward, the latter is necessary.

Another novel aspect of the show was that Levi's was a sponsor, and the company asked every designer to take their jeans, manipulate them in some way, and display them on a mannequin at Levi's booth. Given my history of turning my cousins' denim jeans into bags, this project was right up my alley! So, Levi's sent me a pair of jeans, and I turned them into a corset with my bohemian sleeves. I still have the corset to this day.

COURTESY OF STACY IGEL

Honestly, when I look back at that time, I realize that my most creative design energy was being expressed because I could do anything I wanted and see if it stuck. When you're just starting out as a designer, there's this small window where you have the freedom to let your mind roam in every direction without the burden of being accountable to someone other than yourself. Later on, standing in a booth selling your product can feel like selling your soul. It can be truly grueling—you have to summon every last bit of power from within when buyers pass your booth with barely a glance.

At first, I was sewing and screen printing almost everything myself. Brian also helped me create line sheets, which are documents showcasing your styles with style numbers and pricing for the buyers. We did them in Photoshop with Polaroid pictures he'd taken of me wearing my clothing and based my costs and pricing on our general impression of the marketplace, although my margins were definitely not completely mapped out like they are today. I knew how much I was spending on things like fabric and screening, but I didn't have a factory yet, so it was just a general cost structure and sort of what I knew the market would bear based on shopping and working in stores. Understanding your margins—meaning every bit of money spent on design, fabric, trim, sewing, shipping, and so on—is essential in business, so that you can set your price to cover your expenses and know what you'll actually make on a product. As my friend Alicia Quarles, a journalist and media personality, pointed out: "If you're in a creative field, money doesn't have to be the only motivating factor. Truth and artistry are just as important," which I wholeheartedly believe. However, a bottom line is a bottom line. And, in our case, we were winging it, because I'd never outlined a "real" business structure prior to this show, which was okay for me in the beginning.

My friend and colleague Dana Pollack, who's the CEO and founder of Dana's Bakery, weighed in on this: "Often, entrepreneurs spend so much time working on their business plans that they're not actually working on their business. You have to figure out the first five things you need to accomplish. Check off those things and then start to outline the next five. If you're truly passionate about what you're doing, the most important thing is to keep moving." And that's what I did.

As I continued to prepare for the show, it became clear that I was going to need more hands on deck. Fortunately, a pattern maker I knew in New York City suggested that I start sourcing things in Union City—an awesome artists' colony in New Jersey—because both the rent and hiring staff there were much cheaper than in the Garment Center. He took me out there, and I'll never forget walking into this nearly condemned building, which was basically a sewing plant. There was a fabric guy on one floor, a ribbon guy on another floor, a designer to the left, a sewer to the right, and so on. I couldn't believe it. I thought, *Let me see what the rent is here and maybe I can afford it.*

I ended up finding a place with a small room where I could set up a pattern-making table and an old sewing machine. It was $300 a month, and I could rent it month by month, which was perfect. I was like, *I'm going to do this!* My first desk was a cardboard box, thanks to all the entrepreneurs on the floor who gave me their UPS boxes, and I hired this same pattern maker to be my freelance sewer. He helped me build a pattern-making table out of wood we got from the guys down the hall. And I bought an inexpensive, but sturdy sewing machine from someone else in the building, which I really needed because I'd been sewing everything in my apartment and that machine wasn't going to cut it moving forward.

I would take a tiny bus to Union City from Port Authority every single morning with a laptop strapped to my back. Nine times out of ten, I was the only person on the bus who spoke English as a first language. I had taken Spanish in high school, which turned out to be very useful, since we often watched Spanish soap operas and sports on the bus's little TV as we traveled to and from New York and New Jersey.

Even though the commute was sometimes chaotic, as was setting up all the systems I needed to produce my merchandise, I felt inspired and exhilarated, because I was building my vision.

And then suddenly, on September 11, 2001—the week that the Workshop NY trade show was scheduled to take place—everything changed.

Like most people, that day will be forever etched in my mind and my heart. I'd slept over at Brian's parents' house the night before. He was still working at Chelsea Piers and had already gone into the office. I remember I was getting ready to head to the factory in Union City when Brian's mother came into the room and asked if I'd seen what was going on. I hadn't, because I was busy getting ready for work. She looked at me with a sober expression and said, "Turn on the TV."

Immediately, we saw a video of the first plane crashing into the World Trade Center. We looked at each other and were speechless. It was a moment of total confusion. Then the newscaster came on and—seemingly out of nowhere—a second plane hit the tower in real time. We froze, well aware that Brian was down at Chelsea Piers, and I had friends working at different buildings in New York City. I called Brian to make sure he was okay and then started contacting everybody I knew to make sure no one was in the World Trade Center. Sadly, we had one friend whose sister passed away in the towers, which was devastating. All I could think about was the victims and their families.

It didn't even occur to me to consider what might happen to my own career. Or whether the Workshop NY trade show would still take place. But I knew instantly that whatever happened—given the impact of 9/11 and the overwhelming loss of lives—I had to figure out a way to give back to my city and to the victims' loved ones, whose worlds had been shattered in the wake of such senseless acts of terrorism. That day I resolved to fight even harder for my company, because you never know what tomorrow will bring. I vowed to become a mission brand that would raise awareness through the products I created and also donate money to causes that would help others.

The Workshop NY trade show ended up being postponed until the end of October, but there was another show in Chicago that was taking place earlier in the month, in the Merchandise Mart where I'd worked that summer in high school. My mom suggested that I come home and see if I could take a little spot in someone else's booth, which I thought was a great idea. If nothing else, I felt it would be good preparation for the New York City show.

I flew back to Chicago and ended up in a little corner of another showroom's booth with my BOY MEETS GIRL® and "Ribbon Cinch" collection. I hand-printed cards that said I would be donating proceeds from my first collection to the American Red Cross, specifically to the victims of 9/11 and their families.

The first store in Chicago that bought my shirts, aside from what I'd sold in college, was P45, and after that a few other specialty

stores followed suit. I learned a lot about the geographical aspect of selling to stores from that show, because P45 was in the Halsted area, and there was another store about a mile away that I couldn't sell to due to exclusivity. I was like, *What? Wait a minute! I only sold P45 twelve shirts, how can this be?* Specialty shops back then were very particular about which brands they carried and didn't want the same brand in another shop close by. Of course this makes sense from their perspective, but this kind of limitation makes it hard for young designers to grow.

Something I would tell designers today is not to commit to exclusivities unless the store is buying in bulk or it's the best store on Earth. It turned out okay at the time because I wasn't prepared for bulk production yet, but it was still a valuable lesson learned.

By the time the end of October rolled around, I was armed with this initial experience, and the Workshop NY trade show was ready to launch. As a result of the events of 9/11, there was an incredible spirit in New York. People were ready to be out and about and to support designers. Buyers were excited to have merchandise in their stores, so people could shop. The energy was alive, and the feeling was, *No one is going to take us down!* That was incredibly inspiring to me and motivated me to work even harder to set myself apart.

I was really proud to be a designer in that moment, at such an important show. I recruited a few students from FIT (Fashion Institute of Technology, part of the State University of New York) to work with me, and I even had a model from FIT as well, which was unique, because athleisure/streetwear designers didn't usually showcase T-shirts and sweatpants on models at a trade show—it was more of a high fashion move back then.

There were sixty buyers from all over the world, from Canada to Japan. I was prepared with my samples, everything was displayed, and my mom also flew in to act as a sales rep with me. That was our team. We may not have been seasoned or perfectly

COURTESY OF STACY IGEL

polished, but we were passionate, motivated, and equipped to take on whatever came our way.

What happened next is my mom's favorite story. And this is how she tells it:

Stacy had gone to the ladies' room, and there were three young women who wanted to see her line after noticing a mannequin and model at the front of her booth with her T-shirts on. They had not shown me their badges yet, but I was excited, so I invited them into the booth knowing that Stacy would be back soon. The women said they only had a few minutes, but ended up staying for an hour! Not knowing who they were, I asked the head gal, Tracy, where she was from. When she whispered, "Bergdorf Goodman," my heart skipped a beat! Then Stacy returned to the booth and asked me, "Are they from a good store?" I said, "Honey, that's Mommy's favorite store in the world!" And the rest is history! They loved Stacy's line and bought all the colorways of the cinch and BOY MEETS GIRL® T-shirt collection. I was so very proud of how Stacy sold to them with such expertise of the garment. I'll never forget her laying out the entire line on the floor of the tiny booth and talking them through everything while they listened intently. I knew then and there that this was Stacy's path in life. She was meant to be a fashionista and show the world what it's like to have the knowledge and creativity to get people to understand what she does every day. Hard work, yes, but it was her passion, and she loved every minute of it.

Of course, while all this was going on, my mom kept repeating, in a singsong whisper to me: "Oh my God!! It's Bergdorf Goodman. Oh my God!! It's Bergdorf Goodman. . . ."

I was so embarrassed. I was like, "Calm down, play it cool, and let me continue selling here." But for my mom, who had lived in New York City before she moved to Chicago, Bergdorf was her temple, because it's the ultimate, iconic, luxury department store of all time, and it's been around since 1899. She was so excited, she literally couldn't contain her emotions. For me, coming out of college and being a scouter of vintage clothing, Bergdorf was not my typical shopping destination. Even though I knew it was awesome, it didn't mean as much to me as it did to her . . . at least, not yet.

The important piece of this story is that the "head gal," Tracy Margolies (her official title was buyer, contemporary sportswear), truly believed in what I was doing. She saw something in me and was willing to invest in me, for which I will be forever grateful. I really credit her with putting me on the map as a fashion designer.

Recalling this moment, Tracy, who's now the chief merchandising officer at Saks Fifth Avenue, said: "It's important to support and encourage young designers, or entrepreneurs in any industry, who are just starting out and who like to take chances. If you have the ability to make an impact on someone's career, you should do whatever you can to help them."

I'll never forget sitting in my bedroom that night, totaling my orders from that show, and thinking, *Oh my God, I'm in business!*

As with the trade show in Chicago—once I'd shipped the goods and been paid—I donated a portion of the net proceeds from those orders to the American Red Cross, specifically to the victims of 9/11 and their families, which was the beginning of BOY MEETS GIRL® as an impact brand. From the day I launched after 9/11, I made a promise to myself that, like Tracy, I would always help others by sharing stories and bringing awareness to topics, organizations, and current events that were happening around me.

It was the inspiration from these experiences that allowed me to persevere as I continued to spend late nights in Union City. You have to tell yourself: *I'm doing this. I don't care what time it is. I'm not leaving until everything is done.* Of course I look back now and wonder, *Was I crazy!? How could I get on a bus to Port Authority at midnight all alone?* I guess the simple answer is that the constant work was calming for me. It centered me rather than rattled me.

People often ask if I was "thinking big" during that time; if I was strategizing about how to be a major brand. The truth is that, while that was always my dream, I never made it my focus. It's important, at the outset, to concentrate on what's directly in front of you and take it step-by-step. I'd get one order done, ship it, and then move on to the next order. Those were my immediate goals—to keep my head above water and to move forward. I was literally hanging on tight and living in the moment. I couldn't let myself think too far into the future. There were still a lot of sleepless nights, where I lay awake stressing about everything I wanted to achieve for myself and for my brand, but—again—that kind of stress is soothing for me, because thinking means doing. And a designer's hard work never ends.

I knew it was time to grow my collection and keep differentiating myself in the marketplace, which is challenging, especially when your first collection is a success. I equate it to a musician who releases a hit album and then has to put out a second album. There's a lot riding on your shoulders. My friend Erin C. Hanlon, PhD, research associate professor at the University of Chicago, Department of Medicine, understands the importance of standing out and how that impacts your progress: "Being passionate about what you're doing will help distinguish you from the pack. Enthusiasm can also motivate others, which will lead to success for you and your brand."

For my sophomore effort, I decided to design new shirts that evoked the nostalgic vibe I'd started with. They had felt cutouts of things like cherries, apples, and ducks sewn onto them. It was my hope that Bergdorf Goodman would buy these as well, but producing them ended up being a complete mess, because I had to use multiple factories to complete the final product. One factory was laser-cutting the felt, another factory was cutting the pattern, and yet another factory was sewing the felt onto the cut patterns and assembling the full garment. There was no one-stop shop in the Union City factories, which would have been a much better (and less costly) solution.

I also started creating sweat suits that were made out of a light felt fabric and had these felt appliqués on them. I remember bringing the designs to a cutter before taking them to the sewing plant, and they cut the pattern totally wrong. I had to rebuy all the fabric and have them recut, which was a nightmare and did not help my cash flow. I definitely learned the lesson that some projects are more complicated than others, despite your organization, level of passion, and how hard you work. This is a prime example of how, just when things are going well, something else can go wrong. Learning about production failures early on got my feet wet and prepared me for many future production failures that unfortunately occur often in business. Without learning there can be mistakes and figuring out how to overcome them, you can't move forward.

✓ Be distinctive by knowing that inspiration can come from unexpected places and keeping things fresh with new ideas.

✓ Consider the pros and cons of exclusivity.

✓ Find an industry champion who believes in you.

✓ Focus on what's directly in front of you and take it one step at a time. When you make a mistake, learn from it.

4

As a boss, you need to learn how to do every job
in your company so that you can teach and train
the people who work with you.

When I sold my debut line to Bergdorf Goodman at the Workshop NY trade show in 2001, I was a one-woman show, which meant that there was no job too big or too small for me to undertake—all of it was my responsibility. As an entrepreneur, when you're first starting out, this is often the way it is. You have to understand every aspect of what you do in order to teach others how to work on your behalf, and I sure learned a shitload in the first few days, weeks, and months of building my brand.

As my friend Ami Ankin, who's a producer, actress, and voice-over artist, said: "When you wear many hats and choose to create your own opportunities, you convey how you want to be seen and, also, show that you aren't just the talent, but rather the facilitator. It's empowering to know that you aren't waiting on someone else to give you permission to succeed."

Perhaps the most fundamental duty I carried out was financially supporting my business. Twenty years ago, the buy-now-wear-now trend—which is when you present your products to buyers closer to season, rather than half a year in advance—didn't exist, nor did owning your own e-commerce business or selling on social media, and therefore the actual in-store launch of my products didn't occur until about six months after I sold my line to buyers. In other words, while I was producing the merchandise, I had to fund the business myself, because even when you have a purchase order from a customer, there's no money coming in. You don't get paid until your items land and most of the time it's thirty days after you've shipped them, which is called "net 30 terms." Back then, it was more like forty-five to sixty days, and there were no credit card payments either. Translation: *I need cash fast!*

For a young designer or any budding entrepreneur, this can be a struggle, especially if you get a big order and if your production goes sour or you haven't projected or received financing. In one way, it's exciting and everything you've ever wanted, but in another way it presents a real challenge because you have to produce everything on your own dime. And you don't even know if those pieces are going to sell to customers once the store accepts them. You can go to business school, you can get your feet wet at larger corporations, but it's impossible to understand the foundation of how it all works until you're in it. It's learning by doing.

Of course there are plenty of people who start a company with the help of investors, but I chose not to go that route, primarily because I was reacting to my immediate success and had not outlined a proper business plan. I believe you should outline your goals and address how you're going to fund each step of the process. Just know that while a plan is there to guide you, it can and should be altered based on many variables—namely your sales.

Since I had to act quickly, I opted to apply for a small bank loan and incurred credit card debt that I'd eventually have to reconcile. I did this by borrowing from my bank in Chicago, through my parents, and by using a credit card I'd applied for under my Citibank account in New York City (which had a very low credit limit). I also sought the assistance of a factor to whom I'd been introduced at my first trade show. Factors are people who can finance your orders, lend money to help with production based on your sales, and check your purchase orders to make sure that stores have proof of credit. If you decide to take on a factor, factors will become your best friends.

With my finances in check (for the time being), the line for Bergdorf consisted of my BOY MEETS GIRL® silhouette logo tees; hoodies and sweats; my hippie, flowy, vintage, embroidered sleeves attached to upcycled tees; and my inventive, upcycled ties and ribbon shirts including the Americana ribbons. It had a vibe of uptown-meets-downtown, grunge-meets-dressy, Coco Chanel–meets–Kate Moss–meets–Patti Smith, all intertwined to create an eclectic couture comfort-meets-impact streetwear collection, which is still very much the ethos of my brand.

Lucky magazine collaborated on the in-store launch event, and there were a few other designers launching on the same day, one of whom was the actress Justine Bateman, best known for playing the lead in the movie *Satisfaction* as well as Alex P. Keaton's TV sister on the eighties sitcom *Family Ties*. If you are Gen X, you understand me, and if you are Gen Z, you probably know this show from a vintage tee. I'll never forget when Justine came over and asked me a bunch of questions about the fashion business. I was a total fan of hers and couldn't believe it. I was basically reliving my eighties childhood.

Of course, once the launch event was over, it was time to get down to the actual running of a business, which meant mapping out my business plan to sustain my success and also move forward. It's one thing to live your best life, but when the fanfare subsides, it's back to the grind. Here I was, this twenty-four-year-old girl trying to make a name for myself; and I knew that, to do that, I had to find a way for my pieces to stand out from the pack. More than that, I had to figure out how to make it happen on my own.

Pull it all
together for

this saturday!

MET:

- Justine Bateman
- Tracy Reese
- Marc Vachon
- Rebecca Taylor

- Shin Choi
- Stacy Igel of Deesh
- John Richmond of Richmond Denim

Jennifer Kakon & Scott Richler for Jennifer Scott
Bonnie Held & Abbe Held for Kooba
Lily Rafii & Sulaika Zarrouk for Felix Rey
Jane Shoenborn for Buzz by Jane Fox
Emily and Ashley Green for Greenheads

There are many companies that hire staff to be on the floor in department stores representing their brand. But I didn't have a team of people or even one other employee well versed like me to go represent in Bergdorf Goodman and make sure my product was selling, so I went directly to the source, the salespeople, who were mostly twice as old as I was.

One of the things I learned while I was at Elie Tahari and from other people I'd worked for is that if you put in the effort and the time to talk to the salespeople and guide them so they know your product, then they'll go out of their way to help you.

This is essential, specifically for new designers who can't be at the store every week. I had to concentrate on going out to Union

City to produce the goods, hire people, deal with accounting and picking and packing, outline spreadsheets, and create my next collection.

My good friend and frequent collaborator Hesta Prynn, a well-known New York City–based DJ and author, can attest to the fact that if you're a newbie in almost any industry, you're usually the only point person. She said: "Being part of a start-up, you have to learn how to do every single thing. For example, in my world, you may have to be the artist, the writer, the business and tour manager, the publicist, and the vinyl manufacturer. You need to be able to drive the entire bus by yourself."

Based on this principle, I went to Bergdorf and spoke directly to all the salespeople who worked in the department that sold my clothing. I knew I had to look them in the eyes, explain what my brand and I stood for, and also get to know each of them personally so I could understand their individual strengths and weaknesses. I took everyone through all my pieces and shared that a percentage of the profits would be donated to the American Red Cross in honor of the victims of 9/11 and their surviving family members.

For me, it was necessary that they comprehended not only my professional goals, but also that I'd been running an impact brand from day one and that there would always be a nonprofit piece to it. I told them the story of who I was, where I came from, why I was so excited to launch there, how grateful I was to be in the store, and I went through every stitch of the product, from the thumb holes of my hoodies to the hand-painted shirts to the embroidery and my signature "cinch" shirts. It was so gratifying to see how pumped they became about selling my line.

Basically, I was teaching them how to work for me, even though they didn't actually work for me, so that they would make sure my clothing was on the shelves and that it looked as presentable as possible when I couldn't be there. As an owner and boss, you have to understand how customer service operates and how important that personal touch is when you're trying to stand out. And you have to treat everyone equally, from the picker and the packer to the top salesperson to the president. It doesn't matter who they are, to earn their respect and their belief in your success, every person needs to know that you care about them so they're motivated to represent you and your collection.

After all, as Isaac Mizrahi said in the 2013 documentary *Scatter My Ashes at Bergdorf's*, "If your clothes are not at that place, then they have no future." And my clothes were very much there. They'd sold like hotcakes at the launch event, and I needed to maintain that energy, which was a tremendous amount of pressure and a major reality check.

In addition to that, I started getting a lot of attention in the press and was approached by *Lucky* magazine for its "One to Watch" feature. *Lucky* actually came and shot me in my bedroom where I'd sewn all my own designs. This piece then led to the *New York Times* writing a story on my upcycled, flowy, embroidered, vintage-inspired, hippie-style shirts and my "Ribbon Cinch" shirts. I'd wake up on a Sunday morning to friends and family calling about another newspaper or magazine covering me and my brand, which was both intoxicating and fortunate since I wasn't pitching to media outlets yet. As a result, I was very motivated to continue to learn the publicity piece of pitching one's own business. It was new to me and something I quickly realized I needed to master to keep things in motion. I remembered helping out Zandra Rhodes in London, not only on the design side, but with her lead on public relations.

I wrote in my journal in 1998: "I now know how to write a press release, how to contact important people, what to say, how to organize PR information, and how to stay strong in a tough atmosphere."

Based on that experience, I began creating my own Excel spreadsheets to track which editors were covering me, which styles they were featuring, and which editors had not been in contact with me. I couldn't afford to hire a publicist yet, which was a blessing in disguise. It forced me to stay on top of my own pitches and work directly with these editors so that I could form long-term relationships.

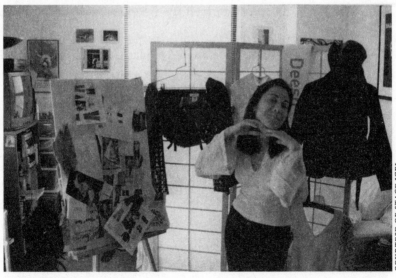

COURTESY OF STACY IGEL

With that said, as integral as public relations is to a brand, I still had to run all the other parts of my business, such as sustaining sales and making money, especially since I was creating inventory for Bergdorf Goodman and other specialty stores who'd begun to place orders. (I was in three hundred to five hundred boutiques across the country over the next few years.)

Everything was happening so fast; I just had to get it done. So, to take some of the work off my plate (and remain cool, calm, and collected), I hired one woman from FIT (the Fashion Institute of Technology) who was part of the crew at my first trade show. I told her I needed help with *everything* and that we'd divvy up the work between the two of us while she traveled back and forth with me from my apartment to the studio in Union City. The only issue was that my apartment (with three roommates) wasn't going to cut it as a makeshift office any longer. It was time for me to find my own place to live in order to advance to the next stage of my business.

As an entrepreneur, working out of your bedroom like I did is a great way to save money in the beginning, but you also have to realize when you've outgrown a specific location (even if it's not your bedroom) and allow yourself the freedom to expand so that you can continue to grow.

Thankfully, I was able to find a bigger place, though I will admit it was insane. There were racks, shelves, computers, boxes, and packing materials everywhere, but I thrive on that kind of chaos. It actually centers me as opposed to flustering me, because I feel like I can stay in control of every area of my business.

Once I had more space, I hired a second full-time employee, an accountant and bookkeeper who came in from time to time, a production assistant, and a bunch of FIT interns who received school credit. Everyone was operating out of my one-bedroom apartment, and I was overseeing all of it with the assistance of a small but solid team.

COURTESY OF STACY IGEL

That doesn't mean there weren't some serious missteps on my part. When you're trying to know it all and do it all, you're bound to make mistakes. And that's okay. You can't be afraid to get things wrong sometimes; it's the only way to learn how to do things correctly. One of the more significant mistakes I made was being too focused on perfection. I wanted our customers to be taken care of *perfectly*. I wanted every email to be answered *perfectly*. I wanted the factory to be paid *perfectly*. I wanted to know my inventory *perfectly*. And I didn't want to disappoint anyone, in any way, which was a lofty and unrealistic goal. Starting a business can be messy. Don't let that mess overwhelm you; instead, embrace it, and find a way to use it to your advantage. I was able to do this by accepting the failures that accompanied my accomplishments and by communicating to others how they could take some of the pressure off me.

My friend Mary Alice Stephenson, founder and CEO of GLAM-4GOOD, whose team has used fashion and beauty to empower more than forty thousand women and their families, echoed this approach: "People can't help you if they don't know what you need. Let people know in every way, every day, how important your work is to you and how and why they can and should support you."

The bottom line is that, while you need to know how to run every aspect of your company yourself, the knowledge and expertise you incur through experience can and should be passed along to those with whom you work so that they can assist you in moving your business forward and achieving the success you desire.

✓ Starting a business can be hectic. Don't let that frenzy overwhelm you. Instead, embrace it and find a way to use it to your advantage.

✓ Map out a business plan, but be flexible to the fact that it will change.

✓ Treat everyone you work with equally in order to earn their respect and their belief in your success.

✓ Put in the time to teach your employees everything you've learned so that they can help you keep moving forward.

5

FIND THE RIGHT PARTNERS

*Choose your partners carefully by making sure they
have the same goals and values as you do.*

When you're first starting out, it's one thing to survive on bank loans and credit card debt. But the reality is that you need more and more money as your company continues to flourish. For the first five years of BOY MEETS GIRL®, the profits from my wholesale store sales were enough to allow me to hire a few employees, pay for my operations, and move into an actual office (within another office)—where I built a little sewing plant—before eventually relocating to a bigger space in the heart of the Garment Center.

COURTESY OF STACY IGEL

But if I wanted to take things to the next level, I had to find a way to increase my funds. The first thing you should know is that there isn't one simple approach to financing your company; it's entirely dependent on what your goals are. You should begin by asking yourself, "How much of my business am I willing to give up if I bring in a partner or even a silent investor? And will this make me happier and more fulfilled than remaining small but profitable as I already am?" You also have to define your vision so that you can select a partner who aligns with what you stand for.

In my case, at this point in my career, I knew I wanted to be *big*—I wanted to be globally known—and to continue giving back to nonprofits by working with activists and cause ambassadors, while educating our consumers about the world around us. I'd gotten by on bootstrapping for long enough, and I couldn't sustain my hamster-wheel pace any longer. Specifically, I needed to hire extra hands, I needed money to put toward marketing and intellectual property, and I needed more help sourcing everything.

With this said, it's really important for entrepreneurs who enlist partners or even venture capital money to understand that when you accept outside funding, you're giving away equity, and the person or company you're giving it to then has a say in your business decisions. Of course it depends on how you structure your deal. For me, it was crucial to maintain creative control of my brand. At the same time, I couldn't do it all on my own anymore.

To give you a better sense of what I'm talking about, in 2005 the *Today* show featured my BOY MEETS GIRL® Coco customized hoodie in their holiday gifting segment. This meant we were customizing any name people wanted over the boy-and-girl logo. It also meant we would likely close our fiscal year way ahead of where I'd projected.

We created a 1-800 number (this was before e-commerce) to accommodate orders once the show aired and had our production streamlined with my local embroidery shop in the Garment Center.

It seemed like an easy enough plan. Unfortunately, the best-laid plans do not always go as intended. The day the segment aired, the *Today* show used my office number rather than the 1-800 number. To make matters worse, this happened during our very busy holiday rush, which was complete pandemonium. I ended up answering the phone myself and taking many of the orders, while pretending I was not the owner of the company. Miraculously, with the help of my small but capable team, we were able to satisfy all our customers before Christmas. Still, I knew that—even though I was able to remain calm—I could *not* sustain things in this manner moving forward.

For this reason, triggered by frustration, I made a decision that I would later regret. I took on my first licensee, Partner A (whom I met through a sales rep of mine), to assist with financing for my company so I could branch out into new areas I couldn't afford on my own. This meant that I owned the intellectual property—the BOY MEETS GIRL® brand name and logo—and the licensee/partner paid me royalties for using my intellectual property. They also took control of production, which meant we could source in other countries and therefore continue to source and make sustainable products. And they made it possible for us to hire additional sales help for department store growth.

As part of our deal, in addition to receiving a royalty as the licensor, I was employed as the creative director of the licensee, which was very rare at the time, though much more common nowadays. Additionally, the licensee took on all my operational expenses and overhead.

Initially, I was thrilled to have the capital to expand my business. I'd been stressed out and exhausted trying to do everything with such a tiny staff, especially since I was engaged to be married and had surrendered any hope of a social life with my fiancé. Sadly, what I'd hoped would be the answer to my prayers ended up being a major regret. By choosing the wrong situation and ignoring the warning signs, I learned the hard way that there are good partners and bad partners.

The main issue was that this licensee brought in some people who wanted to oust me from my own company. They said that I didn't want my brand to succeed, which was absolutely preposterous. I couldn't understand how they could think that I wanted anything but the best for the brand I'd founded and in which I'd invested my blood, sweat, and tears. BOY MEETS GIRL® was my life and my livelihood. Partnering with someone whose goals and creative vision don't align with yours can be detrimental to your success.

As soon as I knew that they didn't trust me or agree with me creatively, it became clear that I couldn't remain in the partnership. Even though we'd done some positive things together, I couldn't work with people who didn't believe in me or my commitment to the brand.

My friend Nicole Purcell, CEO of the Clio Awards, has had experience with this. She said: "Partnerships can be very tricky, but they can also make you a lot stronger, sometimes not in the way you might think. A very valuable lesson is to be careful whom you trust. Don't listen blindly to what anyone says or move forward without research and without surrounding yourself with the right people."

I wrote tons of journal entries on this because it was such an emotional time of trying to figure out how to stay strong when I felt like the only person who could see what was really going on. It drained me physically and mentally, but I was tough, and I promised myself there was no way I was going to let them take me down. Here's one entry that was the impetus for ending the partnership:

I am being taken advantage of and trying to be pushed out of my own brand. You know who wins when that happens— the person who is right! I found an email that was written about me by a sales rep who came to work internally with my licensee. He clearly didn't read his employment manual carefully regarding the licensor's right to monitor emails. Well, this is what he wrote about me: "She is trying to steal the accounts, she tells everyone what to do, and she has no business sense." I am embarrassed, and I am furious. I have been told I do not have thick skin. I beg to differ.

This was a major lesson for me. I learned that when your partners' ideals and intentions don't line up with yours, the relationship won't work. My friend Deb Ross, a licensed acupuncturist who co-owns The Well Center, shared this about professional partnerships: "When you join forces with someone, you have to make sure that you possess the same core values and beliefs. Take time to create your pillars, your inward facing structure, and your philosophy while respectfully and effectively communicating your needs, weaknesses, and strengths to each other. If something isn't working for one of you, have a direct conversation about it. There should be no passive energy. Having this type of depth in a partnership allows you to value each other on so many levels."

Once my term with Partner A was over, I began actively looking for a new partner. I met with a number of industry leaders to see if they wanted to buy a percentage of my brand and take over the current licensing structure. I needed the money and backing and was desperately in search of a company that knew manufacturing and distribution and could provide me with everything I'd been doing myself before Partner A came into the picture. The thing is, as important as it is to do it all in the beginning, it's too hard to do what you do best when you have to do it all forever and always. You need to focus on your strengths to maximize your potential.

Thankfully, in 2007, after a long journey of hustling and pitching just like you might see on *Shark Tank* (PowerPoint presentations, press decks, references, profit and loss statements, and forecasts), I found Partner B. My deal with this partner was structured as a sale of my brand rather than licensing, which means they bought a percentage of my company. I retained ownership and creative control and was employed under the new partnership. For the following three years, Partner B was instrumental in my business's growth. They helped me divide and conquer the current operations of the company and add the element of global distribution, which was a huge step in the right direction. They believed in my creative direction and also challenged it, but I was looking for a challenge. I wanted partners who knew the business, could bring insight to the table, and could open doors for me that I hadn't opened yet.

While Partner B was instrumental in the growth of BOY MEETS GIRL®, by 2010—nearly a decade into my fashion career—I still wasn't entirely content with where I was, business-wise. Despite my successes, I was always thinking about and looking for the next big opportunity and the most efficient way to keep building and improving my brand.

To achieve those goals, I moved on to Partner C. This deal was structured as a buyout of Partner B, as I was able to sell a percentage of Partner B's ownership to Partner C and still remain an owner and in a similar creative role.

Partner C was a multidivisional company worth roughly $300 million with more than twenty brands producing apparel, intimates, bags, socks, watches, and more. It was a much larger organization than the ones I'd aligned myself with in the past, but by the time it came on board, I had far greater insight into what I wanted for BOY MEETS GIRL®. As a result, I stayed with Partner C for five years and made incredible strides in taking my brand to the next level.

Without a doubt, I'd already hit a number of milestones—solo fashion shows, global press, launching in premier specialty and department stores across the country—and now I wanted to expand even further by licensing into product categories, developing digital marketing strategies, finding a bigger showroom, advertising on billboards, and starting an e-commerce site, something that was relatively new then. I wanted everything that the larger brands around me had. With that ambition came a lot of working around the clock, while continuing to keep my cool as I charted new territory—two things that go hand in hand for me.

I truly believe that one of the hallmarks of an entrepreneur is never being completely satisfied with where you are or entirely confident in everything you've achieved. My friend Sophie Elgort, a photographer and director with whom I've worked and collaborated on countless fashion shoots, has experienced this feeling. She said: "Many artists are full of self-doubt and suffer from imposter syndrome, which is when you question your own accomplishments and accolades. The way to get past it is to keep making work and to continue creating. The road to where you want to go is not always linear—you have to pursue various paths, persevere, and learn to not take no for an answer."

I look at my entrepreneurship as constantly trying to find ways to grow, to build, to learn, to give back, and to surround myself with as many interesting, passionate people as possible. Then I can push myself to find the next opportunity. With this in mind, I was able take the knowledge I'd gleaned from my first decade of experience and apply it to the next ten years of my career.

To do this, I made another change in 2015. I'd been with Partner C for five years, which was incredible in terms of growth and distribution, but I knew that I had to spread my wings even further. Thankfully, Partner C was okay with me buying back my company.

After that, Partner D—Munir Mashooqullah—entered the picture; we'd met because his company was a sourcing agent for my prior partners. Munir is the founder of Synergies Worldwide. He'd built a global sourcing company in the way of products and production and also had international experience, which was exactly what I wanted—to work with someone who possessed the same ideology as I did, moving forward. He was a mentor to me on my journey and someone I looked up to. He always believed in me, which is key when you're joining forces with someone and bringing them into your fold.

I knew if I wanted everything I'd been building to be implemented as I'd imagined, I needed someone to help me gain even greater global awareness—someone who had the same sustainable goals as I did and a direct line to manufacture any product anywhere around the world from Pakistan and Turkey to Bangladesh, India, and China. Sourcing and production had always been the hardest part of my business, and now that I knew how to find a manufacturing house, make tech packs, create samples, and follow through with everything on the production end, this new partnership would be a welcome complement.

Fortunately, Munir and I had a great connection, and we both knew we'd work well together. He believes: "You have to look for partners who have the ability to innovate and keep their brand relevant in the current marketplace. You should let the founder run his or her business, while you offer the synergy of supply chain and financial management in order for everyone to maximize their potential."

I'm pleased to say that Munir and I did realize our potential together. As an entrepreneur, it's essential to keep in mind that taking on a partner is never perfect or exactly how you envisioned it—you have to find ways to make it work that benefit both of you in the long run.

✓ There are various options for funding your business; you have to figure out what's most effective for the continued growth of your brand.

✓ As important as it is to do it all in the beginning, you can't maintain that level of control forever. You need to focus on your strengths to maximize your potential.

✓ Remember that when you accept outside funding, you're giving away equity and the person or company you're giving it to then has a say in your business decisions.

✓ Avoid making choices triggered by urgency or frustration, or you'll regret them later.

6

THINK OUTSIDE THE BOX

Success comes in many forms, and—with anything you do in business—you have to constantly reinvent yourself.

As an entrepreneur and fashion designer, I'm always thinking about how I can stay ahead of the trends and gain visibility for my brand by doing things that will surprise consumers in the best way possible.

I've found that the most effective ways to do this are by getting my products into the hands of the right people, creating partnerships with a variety of businesses, and collaborating with philanthropic organizations. I'm very lucky that, throughout the course of my career, I've had the chance to do all these things many times over.

One of the first big opportunities along these lines was when my BOY MEETS GIRL® signature iconic logo tee was worn by Lorelei, actress Lauren Graham's character on the cult classic TV show *Gilmore Girls*. Because I always made it a point to be in touch directly with editors and stylists and I traveled to Los Angeles a couple times a year for trade shows, when I reached out to the *Gilmore Girls* stylist, she invited me to the set. I even got to thank Lauren Graham for rocking my clothing.

This was before mainstream social media existed. Suddenly everyone wanted this T-shirt, and all eyes were on BOY MEETS GIRL®. Back then, the power of TV was similar to the influence of digital platforms today.

The visibility from *Gilmore Girls* led to *America's Next Top Model* doing a runway piece on their show in which all the models wore BOY MEETS GIRL®, which was surreal. I'll never forget when Patricia Field, costume designer for *Sex and the City*, had her buyer Sushi (that really is his name) called to tell me that he was going to dress all the *ANTM* women in my clothing, and that they were going to practice their struts in my skirts and logo camisoles. Now, *that* was a moment.

Of course, once you've been on two major TV shows, more retailers and people want to buy and wear your pieces. My designs were picked up at a hot store called Intuition in Los Angeles, and Paris Hilton went in and bought a BOY MEETS GIRL® hoodie. Then Kimora Lee Simmons wanted one, and it became this amazing ripple effect.

Building on this momentum, I decided to find other distinctive methods of making my brand stand out. One was to partner with the Cooper Square Hotel, which had recently opened in Manhattan's East Village (it's now the Standard Hotel). My friend Evan Altman, then the head of marketing at the hotel, mentioned an idea to be in their minibars, which I absolutely loved. I thought, *How great would it be if guests of the hotel could open their minibar and buy not only a little bottle of vodka and a bar of chocolate, but also a piece of clothing?* It was precisely the off-the-beaten-path concept I wanted for my brand and, before long, my signature tees with the BOY MEETS GIRL® logo were available in every room's minibar.

To commemorate this innovative approach, this blurb ran on the website Guest of a Guest, with the headline, "Everything Except 'Hookers and Drugs' at the Cooper Square Hotel":

Cooper Square Hotel manager Klaus Ortlieb, an Ian Schrager alum, believes in, "[providing] everything the guests want except hookers and drugs." Fitting right into this generous hospitality philosophy are the makeup, clothing, and jewelry available in the hotel's guest room minibars. Bobby Flay, Stephanie March, Jason Patrick, Happy Massee, and BOY MEETS GIRL's Stacy Morgenstern Igel ascended to the hotel penthouse yesterday to glimpse the unveiling of these and other playful amenities while taking in the incredible view. Now that you can get everything you need without leaving the privacy of your hotel room, the only thing left to ask for is maybe some summer weather.

The ability to think outside the box with projects like this was ahead of the market—and this collaborative initiative opened up a general concept that is still prevalent today. People can now buy clothing and beauty products from machines at the airport too. The lesson here is that even when something may seem like a small enterprise, it may pave the way for far greater evolution and even more diverse prospects.

On the heels of my success with the Cooper Square Hotel, I was approached by Soho House—a private members' club with locations all over the world—to design uniforms for the staff at their New York location. I was excited because I knew that the extra exposure would really elevate my brand. I also felt it was a great way to learn a new market and attract more buyers. On top of dressing the employees, I did an interview series and photographed a few of the staff members as a means of better understanding who they were. It was important for me to be able to tell their stories through the designs that we had been doing since inception.

One of the women I spoke to was the up-and-coming actress Ashley Brown, who was waiting tables at Soho House while auditioning on her off days. Now, Ashley is known as Novi Brown, the star of Tyler Perry's *Sistas* on BET.

While the glitz and glamor of having my designs featured on TV and in hotels was fun and lucrative, I continued building the impact and mission of our brand by bringing awareness to our consumers with several nonprofits making change. One was the Young Survival Coalition (YSC) in support of breast cancer. As a business owner, it's necessary to pay it forward, especially when the causes are near and dear to your heart. For me, there have been many of these through the years, but at that moment, I was focused on breast cancer awareness because my grandmother had died from it. I am grateful that it didn't take her life until she was much older, and I wanted to learn more about why women under the age of forty were being afflicted with the same disease. I was introduced to the YSC through my friend Lynn Bermont, whose stepsister found out she had breast cancer at thirty-seven. Thanks to Lynn, I went to one of the Theory stores for my first meeting with YSC to learn and see how I could become involved.

That's where I met a young woman named Kristen Martinez, who had stage IV breast cancer and became one of my dearest friends for many years before she passed away in 2010. At the time, Kristen had just gone through chemotherapy and radiation, and she was still so full of life. She was game for anything, as I always am, and we worked on the In Living Pink (ILP) gala together, a phenomenal process. The more my friendship with Kristen grew, the more I wanted to help raise awareness. She convinced me to become a chair with her on several more ILP events, and it was truly one of the most impactful collaborations I've ever experienced. During this time, Kristen asked me to team up with Urban Outfitters (where she worked) to develop a product that would donate back to the YSC. We cocreated a tote bag made of natural fibers that had the BOY MEETS GIRL® logo with breast cancer awareness ribbons inside it. It was sold in every Urban Outfitters store, and we raised more than $15,000 for the YSC.

Since then, my advocacy for the YSC has not stopped. And that's how I started working with Urban Outfitters, who later came to me again to do a special BOY MEETS GIRL® collaboration, because of Kristen. After that collaboration, they wanted to do a designer collection with me in the form of a sustainable line with recycled yarns and lyocell, which takes the cellulose from wood pulp, to be exact. The pulp is broken down into recyclable chemicals and spun into fibers that are used to make yarn, which can then be turned into clothing and gear. Making lyocell doesn't require toxic chemicals, and, compared to cotton, lyocell has the potential to use less than half as much water during production. Bringing this sustainability to the forefront was new for Urban Outfitters, which is why our partnership was so important. Kristen was proud of these efforts, and my goal has been to carry on her legacy through advocacy and bringing awareness to the cause every day.

But my chosen responsibility as an impact brand and my philanthropic endeavors that require thinking outside the box did not stop there. Through becoming involved in social media in its beginning stages, I began to notice that there was a lot of cyberbullying going on. Since BOY MEETS GIRL® was selling to so many different age groups, I felt it was my duty to educate our consumers on cyberbullying and how to prevent it. I couldn't understand why such a small number of people were talking about such an important cause, so I reached out to the National School Climate Center (NSCC) about its BullyBust program to learn more and help in any way I could. As it happened, I was then introduced to a young actress named Sammi Hanratty, who's still a dear friend of mine.

I was working with a lot of young actresses at the time, and one of the publicists said to me: "We'd love to introduce you to Sammi. We know you're engaged with the National School Climate Center's BullyBust program, and we're hoping maybe she can become an advocate with you to spearhead their mission, because this is what she's doing as an actress."

I thought that was a great idea and would draw even more attention to cyberbullying and bullying of all kinds. So, Sammi and I came together and designed a shirt that had the BOY MEETS GIRL® logo, with a shadow of people standing up inside of it. We collaborated with Bloomingdale's to benefit the National School Climate Center's BullyBust program, which Sammi remembers well: "When I was thirteen, I played the main character in a movie called *An American Girl: Chrissa Stands Strong.* Chrissa was the 2009 'Girl of the Year' for American Girl and her story revolved around school bullying. After filming a movie on this important topic, I knew I wanted to use my voice to do something to help bring awareness to end school bullying. At the same time, NSCC and Stacy were collaborating on a campaign for BullyBust.org. After meeting Stacy and seeing her vision and compassion, it made it a no-brainer for me to come on board. My role was to help educate youth on the importance of standing up for one another to stop bullying."

Sammi and I sold shirts from New York and Chicago to Los Angeles and everywhere in between. All the girls who were buying her doll and watching her movie were learning about how to protect themselves and how to stop bullying. This was before the major anti-bullying campaigns that we see now, and we had lines around the corner in the Bloomingdale's kids section. Everyone wanted to meet Sammi and also to learn about BOY MEETS GIRL®.

Another major coup for my business, as far as distinguishing ourselves in the eye of the consumer, was when I was approached by a woman named Nancy Ganz who'd founded a company called Fashion Fantasy Game (FFG), and constructed an online game in which you could dress your avatars (this was way before the hundreds of dress-up/fashion mobile apps available today). Nancy was the kind of fierce woman leader I love to be aligned with, and—like me—she was all about creating ahead of a trend. We decided to collaborate in a couple of ways. The first thing was that players of her FFG could log in, go "shopping," and style their avatars in BOY

MEETS GIRL® logo hoodies. Virtual innovation! Additionally, we ran a contest where players submitted their avatars' looks, and we selected winners. The winners then came to shadow me for a week and learn about the fashion business, which I was excited about, knowing I was giving back to the younger generation.

Next we approached Bloomingdale's, which had been heavily involved with my anti-bullying efforts and also carried my full collection, and we facilitated customers' ability to not only dress their avatars through FFG, but also to shop the BOY MEETS GIRL® hoodie for themselves on Bloomingdale's website. It was this whole new wave of how to reach the consumer and the beginning of gaming and fashion coming together.

These are the types of collaborations that keep an entrepreneur moving and revolutionizing within an industry. As I said, success comes in many forms, but it also comes with challenges. Each of these projects had a different production house, a different manager, and multiple people with whom I was communicating. So, yes, you will have major highs in your career, though they're far from the entire picture. To maintain progress, you have to embrace these highs and also be able to handle the challenges that accompany them with grace and composure.

✓ Success may take unexpected forms. Learn to welcome the unknown.

✓ Collaborating with different businesses, artists, and philanthropic organizations that align with your mission will help you garner visibility for your brand.

✓ Even when something seems like a small opportunity, it may pave the way for greater evolution.

✓ Exploring new markets will attract new consumers.

7

LIVE THE DREAM

*It's important to celebrate the milestones in
your career in order to stay motivated and keep
the momentum going.*

While the life of an entrepreneur is a constant roller-coaster ride and a tremendous amount of hard work, there comes a time to rejoice in your accomplishments and live your dream. For me, that dream was to produce my first solo runway show in 2009—the real-world version of the ones I'd put on in my home as a child.

There are definitely schools of thought within the fashion industry that say a designer's debut show should come earlier in his or her career, but that wasn't my path, and that's okay. Whatever step you're taking in your journey, it has to be right for you and make sense for your brand. What made sense for me was selling to retail stores, collaborating with different companies and charitable organizations, and licensing in other countries. I would not send BOY MEETS GIRL® down an official runway until I felt ready in my gut.

My friend Katya Libin, cofounder of HeyMama, echoed this sentiment: "As an entrepreneur, often, you have to move a bit slower to achieve success in certain areas, which may sound counterproductive when you're thinking about growing a business, but it's better not to rush to get to a specific point. You have to possess the confidence to believe in yourself and take that huge leap of faith."

Once I started to feel ready, Nicole Purcell—now a friend and current president of the Clio Awards—approached me with an alluring opportunity. At the time, *ELLE* magazine had covered BOY MEETS GIRL® and our collaboration with Soho House, a club for creatives. *ELLE* was also a partner with Rock Media, where Nicole was president, and she was looking for designers to join her new show in Los Angeles. A lot of brands were showcasing at Fashion Week. She also said that she had an opportunity for BOY MEETS GIRL® to do a solo show there. I agreed immediately, knowing that my brand was ready to have its moment on the catwalk.

As with any major production, putting on a fashion show is no joke. Fortunately, my sponsor Rock Media booked the venue, covered much of the cost, and also hired six security guards to manage the mayhem, because it is absolute chaos. Backstage was crammed with models, their clothes pinned in at least ten different directions. Hair and makeup people flitted about like frantic dragonflies, and everyone was chatting at once. The models were all lined up and needed to know where to go and when to start moving. It was constant scrambling, running back and forth, and making sure everything was being executed according to my vision, all while I was being interviewed by press for future coverage. We also had a DJ who was prepping the music with me at the same time. And, while all this was going on, I was acting as a cheerleader, telling everyone that they were doing a good job, overseeing each ensemble I'd prepared with my co-stylist, Ali Lang, and encouraging the models, telling them that they looked fabulous. The best way to describe the madness behind the scenes is that it was like being in New York City, in the middle of Times Square, with a ton of activity going on around you and billboards flashing.

One thing a lot of people may not realize is that when designers do shows, their collections have to be much bigger than a regular line. You can't feature just a few items, because not all the pieces will be picked up by stores. In light of this, I really wanted to put my best foot forward and wow the buyers, editors, producers, publicists, and all the other guests with a considered, artistic, and impactful presentation. And since the theme was rock 'n' roll, I knew I had to go big or go home.

I'd never done anything on this scale before, but I didn't let that stop me. You can't allow fear of the unknown to get in your way; otherwise it will stunt your progress. I'll never forget the thrill of the lights coming up, the music blaring, and the models bursting onto the stage, as I peered through the curtain at the thousand attendees, including my parents and friends who were beaming with pride. Of course the seating chart for a thousand people is a beast in and of itself. When you look at the RSVPs and you see buyers, celebrities, family members, and friends, you want to fit everybody in the front row, but you can't. It's like arranging seating for your wedding—you don't want to offend anyone, only this is harder because it's straight rows, not round tables, and there's a definite status attached to being front and center. But, at some point, you have to release control and let the show go on.

An article by Erin Barajas in *Apparel News* captured the vibe perfectly:

> Designer Stacy Igel looked to 1980s glam-band rockers for inspiration for the Spring 2010 collection for her line, Boy Meets Girl, which bowed on the runway on Oct. 30 at Rock Fashion Week at the Petersen Automotive Museum. The New York–based designer co-opted the bad boys' skin-tight jeans, band T-shirts and slashed aesthetic and mixed it with a Cyndi Lauper-style affinity for lace, flouncy skirts and off-the-shoulder shirts. Igel

enlisted the help of six woman musicians (whose fortes range from hip-hop and soul to pop) to help her create the musically inspired collection. The six singers will be featured in Boy Meets Girl's Spring 2010 lookbook.

As a result of that show, when I got back to New York, a lot of new stores picked up my line, generating a significant amount of sales for the company. Of course, this isn't always the way. It's important to note that not everything you do brings you a return on investment in terms of immediate financial profit. However, visibility is another ROI, which could lead to more monetization in the longer run.

After the show in Los Angeles, that's exactly what happened. A group of people producing fashion shows in New York wanted to do a collaborative event with me and a few other brands, sponsored by Starbucks in conjunction with STYLE360. Because I'd featured incredible musicians in my campaign for the Los Angeles show, the manager for the band Neon Trees also got in touch and wanted to be involved. I loved that idea because it would be my first fashion show to open with live musicians performing—another celebration of the ethos of BOY MEETS GIRL®, which is to join artists of all kinds.

David Manning, the founder and executive producer of STYLE360 and a ten-year veteran in the music industry before he shifted into events and public relations, deeply understood the mission of my brand. "Music and fashion are very similar, because they both involve creative people moving at a fast pace," he said. "There's always an adrenaline rush in making the impossible possible."

That adrenaline rush, blooming from the chaos of my job, is precisely what keeps me moving. For business owners, it's important to rejoice in your career highs as a means of inspiring future achievements. I wrote the following journal entry as a way to remember what it felt like to celebrate everything I'd accomplished:

I keep pinching myself.

I haven't stopped my work ethic to build the ultimate dream.

I was destined to be doing exactly what I'm doing.

By far the most significant nod to the growth of BOY MEETS GIRL® came when I was asked to do my first solo show in New York, the place where it all started. Not only that, but—through my music industry connections—I recruited Natasha Bedingfield to give an acoustic performance on the runway and actress Taryn Manning to spin at the after-party.

It was an honor when Natasha came to my office prior to the show so we could get to know each other, and I could style her in my designs. When you're collaborating with other artists, it's important to work with them directly, so you can make sure they're comfortable. You can't just randomly hire someone with whom you have no connection; it won't feel organic or authentic. You want to make sure the artists you're collaborating with believe in the same things you do. My friend and musician Jarina De Marco has experienced this firsthand. She said: "The most important asset in any career is authenticity. Staying authentic ensures that your work comes from a real place and is fully aligned with who you are, which people recognize and get excited about."

One other event that was momentous for BOY MEETS GIRL® was "The Americana Show," commemorating the company's ten-year anniversary and honoring those we lost on September 11, 2001. I wanted to change up the traditional runway show vibe and create an intimate event as we reflected on the past decade. So, we selected the club Avenue, a smaller venue in Manhattan's Chelsea neighborhood. The pop duo The Veronicas gave a spirited acoustic performance, and NBA player Dwight Howard and tennis star Victoria Azarenka hosted the night with me.

I re-created old pieces from our archive in red, white, and blue to represent the history of my decade in fashion. I tie-dyed and

ANNA THIESSEN PHOTOGRAPHY

spray-painted many of those pieces as well and added some of my ribbon trims from the beginning of time. The models had red, white, and blue lips with stars and stripes and big, funky hair. It was a celebration of life.

As with my first trade show in New York City after 9/11, this particular Americana show was about persevering and making an impact on the world. It was also about taking a moment to salute all the hard work we'd invested over the last decade. We felt, at our core, that this hard work would allow us to keep moving, building, and growing.

✓ Although entrepreneurship involves many highs and lows, don't forget to celebrate your accomplishments and live your dream.

✓ Whatever step you're taking in your journey, it has to be right for you and make sense for your business.

✓ You can't let fear of the unknown get in your way; it will stunt your progress.

✓ Every accomplishment isn't an immediate return on investment in terms of financial profit, but it might be an ROI in other ways, which will lead to monetization in the longer run.

8

PROTECT YOUR ASS—ETS

*In business, it's essential to safeguard your original
ideas so that competitors don't copy you.*

As with most industries, in the field of fashion, you need to protect your intellectual property—a.k.a. your assets—such as trademarks for your brand name and logo in multiple classes of goods and services, patents, trade dress (overall product image), and copyrights for certain design and product packaging elements. Then you have to safeguard these assets all over the world so that other companies don't copy something you've created.

Often, new business owners avoid doing this because it can be expensive or because they think they don't have anything worth replicating yet, but I'm here to tell you that's a mistake.

My best advice is to hire a good lawyer, right from the start, who knows about intellectual property, as that area of law can be counterintuitive and confusing. Speak by phone to at least three lawyers to get a feel for each as a person and an understanding of their experience, and also ask for a couple references. The actual cost to file a trademark application covering one class of goods (for example, Class 025 covers apparel, footwear, headwear, etc.) in the United States Patent and Trademark Office is currently about $350, so keep that in mind when considering the quotes. Because a lawyer can be costly, you should do preparation beforehand by conducting your own search on the United States Patent and Trademark Office website (www.uspto.gov) and, if an international scope is important, on the European Union Intellectual Property website (www.tmdn .org). Develop a list of questions before your first call. Ask open-ended questions and let the lawyer talk; you'd be surprised by how much information lawyers are willing to share. Make sure to get a quote in writing (and make sure you understand what does and does not come with that quote), and then compare notes between your three prospects. Don't be afraid to call back and clarify if necessary.

It is possible to conduct a search and file your own copyright and trademark application, but in my experience the cost of engaging a lawyer to deal with intellectual property, draft templates, and bounce ideas off of at the start of something new is less than the price of cleaning up the inevitable mess that results from doing things you don't understand and haven't been trained for.

When I started to build the name BOY MEETS GIRL® and our logo became more widely known, almost immediately people began replicating it and using our name in advertisements, which meant I had to spend time sending cease-and-desist letters and threatening lawsuits. I'll be honest—those legal bills ate me alive. I didn't have the money that big fashion labels like Donna Karan or Ralph Lauren had or a budget that accounted for guarding my growing brand. Until it was actually happening to me, I had no idea what a financial burden it would be. I was operating in my own world of inventing, crafting, and creating, and then, without warning, I'd find out that a brand in another country was using the name BOY MEETS GIRL® without permission.

I'd never been to law school, and legal intellectual property and trademark analysis weren't covered in my small business certificate classes at the University of Wisconsin, so I had to learn as I went. A perfect example of this is the "Ribbon Cinch" shirt I invented when I first launched, because getting a design patent for something like this is extremely complicated. Merriam-Webster defines a patent as "a writing securing for a term of years the right to exclude others from making, using, or selling an invention." Along these lines, there's also something called a trade dress, which protects all elements used to promote a specific service or product, including packaging. Again, this entails a lot of money and a lot of research.

So, when my "Ribbon Cinch" shirt released at Bergdorf Goodman in 2002 and was being featured in major magazines and newspapers, like the *New York Times*, and seen on celebrities (one of the characters on the TV show *Felicity* wore it, as did the lead on *Bend It Like Beckham*), things started getting dicey, which is the opposite of what I expected, given this amazing exposure.

A famous fashion designer's daughter had a reality show and, on the show, she wore one of my cinch shirts into her dad's office. Normally, I'd be thrilled to have one of my pieces showcased on television by the daughter of a huge designer, but they weren't talking about me or my brand on that episode. Instead, she was reviewing her dad's line, while wearing my shirt, which to me was super cool at the time, until . . .

As a new designer in the market, I didn't know much about design patents or trade dress, but I had created this special "cinch" where the location of the gathered ribbon was sewn at the same place each time and then gathered in a way to hold the ribbon so it looked like a fan around the breast area, flattering all shapes and sizes. I worked with my head pattern maker and the team at my factory in Union City, and there were only a few sewers whom I allowed to produce the product and who were privy to the pattern. Seeing this major designer (along with a few others) copy it was crazy and very frustrating. It was also infuriating that they were able to set a cheaper retail price than I was since they could mass-produce it overseas in places like Hong Kong and Peru. In turn, I was still creating in my domestic factories with special care, because I'd just started my business. I didn't know about volume sourcing at that time. I had friends sending me photos and buying samples, saying, "These people ripped you off!" I couldn't believe it. I felt my hands were tied since I wasn't in a position to sue these fashion giants. It would have buried me. But, in the same vein, I couldn't imagine letting them get away with it.

Fueled by frustration, I spoke to my lawyer who warned me that going after these big-name designers would incur a very hefty bill. This was extremely disheartening to hear; I'd created this design from scratch and really put my heart and soul into it, and I didn't have the funds to protect myself. Yes, it was flattering that I'd conceived something that was so desirable to these industry standouts, but not flattering enough to make it okay. And, unfortunately, unlike the digital/social media world of today, I had no option to engage in a coordinated social media shaming campaign.

Eventually, I did get a trade dress on the cinch shirt (on the Supplemental Register with the idea that the cinch could acquire distinctiveness over time). And, clearly, I succeeded and continued to build my brand regardless. Still, it was a major learning curve that I hadn't expected and that a lot of business owners don't anticipate.

As I said, if you're an entrepreneur starting your own company, you have to be very aware of protecting your intellectual property. Don't wait to register your name because it costs a few hundred dollars. You need to be able to dedicate resources and protect your marks. A dollar spent today protecting your marks will save you ten dollars when a thief tries to swoop in and steal what you've built. As my friend Nancy A. Schuster, who's a serial entrepreneur, advised: "Trust your gut. If you have a good idea, don't tell anyone immediately, just execute it. And when you do take your space, own it." I agree with this completely. Still, once your idea is out in public, copycats will come out of the woodwork when you least expect it.

And it's not just the larger companies. During the period when I was doing a lot of trade shows, I hired a showroom that provided sales reps within the firm to help me sell. I worked very closely with one of the reps, and she got to know me personally. She asked me all of these great questions about my line and why I'd created it. I thought she was a true partner on my team.

Well, guess what? She arrived at a show the next season (no longer working at that showroom) with her own line that looked *exactly* like mine! My buyers approached me and said: "Stacy, she has a logo just like yours on her hang tags. She's also using ribbons that are strikingly similar to yours."

I was in shock. I couldn't believe how duplicitous she was. I mean, this woman literally sat with me selling my line and then ripped me off! I thought we were in it together, and a season later she was stabbing me in the back. If you don't have a stomach of steel and you're unable to channel your calm amid this kind of chaos, you can really fail.

My friend Pamela Pekerman, founder of Hustle Like a Mom, weighed in on this: "Entrepreneurship is creating something out of nothing, and—because of that dedication—there are a lot of frustrating moments. You have to learn to combat that frustration by going inward for a hot minute. There's an expression that says something like, 'You can't see your reflection unless you stop and look at the water.' This is important to always keep in mind."

Of course, this is easier said than done sometimes, and you might feel like saying "fuck it" and walking away, because it's not fun and it's not glamorous, especially when you had thought these people were your colleagues and your friends. This woman, who was originally hired to promote my brand, had the audacity to look me in the eye and think there would be no consequences.

I felt like screaming: *Hello! Do you not see me?! Do you not understand that this is something I've put endless hard work and a load of money into? Do you not get that this product is protected?*

The lesson here is that you can't sit back and let people exploit you; you have to take action. I asked my lawyer to send a cease-and-desist letter to remind her that she'd been a sales rep of mine and had sold my line before duplicating it as though it were hers. She had a strong lawyer, too, who sent back some bullshit history of her silhouettes and other erroneous "proof" they thought would support her case, though I didn't let that unnerve me. I channeled my calm during this chaotic circumstance with the knowledge that justice would prevail, which it did. This victory may seem minor, but it wasn't. I got her to stop, and I set a precedent that if someone tried to impersonate my brand, I'd go after them with guns blazing.

While winning felt great, it didn't take away the sting of being deceived by someone I trusted. Regardless, I refused to let her betrayal stand in my way. To this day I can't understand how any creative people could do something like this and still be able to live with themselves.

As a business owner, you will experience these types of disturbances to your progress. Instead of letting them thwart you, you have to keep your cool, maintain a positive attitude, and continue to push forward.

If there's anyone who truly understands this struggle, it's my friend Wendy Starland—singer, songwriter, and music producer—who discovered and developed Lady Gaga. Here's some wisdom Wendy passed along for budding entrepreneurs: "In order to uphold your professional interests, you have to be smart. Surround yourself with people you trust, and protect both yourself and your work with legal documents specific to your industry."

In the end, even if it seems like you're getting ahead of yourself, you'll be happier and more successful if you take the necessary precautions from the start. Just because you may play by the rules, that doesn't mean everyone else will.

✓ New business owners often avoid protecting their assets because it can be expensive, or because they think they don't have anything worth replicating. That's a mistake. Invest in a good lawyer if possible.

✓ Copycats will come out of the woodwork when you least expect them. Be very cautious about whom you trust.

✓ You can't sit back and let people exploit you; you have to take action.

✓ If you don't have a stomach of steel, the chaos of being imitated by a competitor will consume you.

9

BE THE BOSS

*Being the boss can be a daunting prospect, but you have
to lead with confidence and leave emotion out of it.*

Running the show isn't always easy, and it typically comes with a variety of challenges. To be an effective leader, it's important to have clear boundaries with your employees. However, this should be balanced with creating a work environment in which employees feel valued and their efforts appreciated. Some qualities of a great boss include grace under pressure, decisiveness, and empathy. Clear communication and a culture of listening, with the understanding that the leader makes the final decision, are also essential in the workplace.

On the flip side, people-pleasing, overfamiliarity, and lack of clear consequences/accountability for negative actions can create long-term issues, even if your actions may feel right in the moment.

In my case, I was only twenty-four when I launched my brand, and many of my staff members were the same age as me or even older. I didn't always possess the confidence I should have had as a boss. And I definitely made a number of errors, including letting my personal feelings get in the way of my professional decisions.

While I'd worked for a number of strong woman leaders and had witnessed their dedication firsthand, that didn't necessarily train me to be a boss myself. It's not something you can be taught. Learning how to lead comes with experience, and it's taken me twenty years to fully educate myself on how to manage people in the most effective way.

The first and most fundamental thing to keep in mind when you own a company is that no employee will be as committed as you are, because no employee knows everything that needs to be done to steer a company successfully. When you're in the trenches, getting product out the door, returning emails all day long, and just trying to keep up with the lightning-speed pace, you can't assume that everyone is on the same page as you. At the end of the day, it's your business, not theirs. I do believe that there are those truly special people who will treat your business like it's theirs and really care about the success of the brand—and those are the people I've always tried to hire—but you can't expect to find an endless supply of such people.

As a business owner, I've always been someone who wants to say yes to everyone and everything. You want product? Okay! You need a hundred more hoodies? Consider it done! I'm perfectly happy to work deep into the night to make sure that I deliver. The thing is, even if you're okay with staying up until two o'clock in the morning, it's not necessarily appropriate to be firing off emails to your staff at that time.

When I first started, people weren't really corresponding on cell phones, so my employees would arrive at the office every morning to a barrage of lengthy emails from me, which felt overwhelming for them. Since I worked 24-7, I expected my staff to work 24-7 too. I didn't understand why they weren't emailing me back after hours and why they didn't possess the same urgency for getting things done as I did. I've since learned to respect my employees' out-of-office time, because I now understand that allowing them the opportunity to reset and rejuvenate means they'll arrive at work the next day feeling unencumbered and with a positive attitude.

Two other big mistakes I've made as a boss are trying to be good friends with my employees and allowing my emotions to affect my professional relationships. Unfortunately, these were both very hard lessons for me to digest and implement. When you manage staff, you can't be a people pleaser, or make everyone who works for you happy at all times; that's simply not realistic.

This isn't to say that you can never have fun. Sure, there are companies, mostly in the tech world, that have common rooms with Ping-Pong tables and other communal games. Occasionally I took my employees out to dinner or to a cool fitness class as a means of building camaraderie, but you can't make a habit of hanging out with the people who work for you outside the office. In other words, your subordinate should not be your yoga buddy.

Add to that the fact that you can't let your personal life impact your ability to spearhead your team. Everyone is human, so naturally there will be instances when you're grumpy, stressed out, or angry with your significant other, a friend, or a family member. When I'm in this mode, I have the tendency to become a control freak, which leads me to micromanage everyone around me and send random Google documents that everyone has to fill out. Over the years, I've taught myself that this kind of behavior doesn't lead to respect and that I'm a much more effective boss when I remain calm rather than being oversensitive. This allows me to get things done without worrying that I've unintentionally offended someone.

My friend Christina Rice, chief experience officer at OMNoire, has had plenty of experience with this. She said: "When you're at the helm, you have to remember that the people who work for you are watching what you do. You have to ask yourself what feels right in any given moment and try not to let fear, insecurity, or anxiety get in the way. And leave emotions out of your decision making, no matter how agonizing it may be."

Still, for me, it was an uphill battle. I expected that every person I hired would stay with me for twenty years, but—again—that's not entirely realistic. I should say that, as a general rule, I've had exceptional longevity with my employees, so it's not out of the question to maintain that level of devotion, especially when you put in the effort. My friend and collaborator Sarah Andelman, founder and former creative director of the store colette, offered this advice: "In order to achieve loyalty from your employees, you have to be present and keep your team motivated, excited, and inspired."

I fully agree with Sarah, and that's how I've always tried to operate, although, with any business, there will inevitably be turnover. There will be someone who wants a bigger salary (when you can't afford to pay it), or someone who wants to be his or her own boss and take on a new challenge, all of which is completely reasonable.

It's okay to allow give and take, as long as you're not a pushover. I've let people work from home under special circumstances or take an extended vacation if we've come off a big event. The problem is that there's usually someone who will take advantage of this kind of generosity. For example, I once granted an employee extra time out of the office, and when she came back to work, she told me she was moving to another state and gave me two weeks' notice. In this case, it was a life circumstance on her part, but it definitely taught me not to take these things too personally and that, as a boss, there's only so much I can do when something like this happens.

A lot of people say that all employees are easily replaceable, but I don't believe that's the case. If you've trained someone to do things your way, invested your time in him or her, and cultivated a relationship, you can replace that employee, but it doesn't mean it'll be simple, especially if you run a small business. When someone resigns, it's always challenging to regroup, but in order to remain calm, you have to tell yourself that if you found someone great the first time, you'll find someone great again. It may be an opportunity to reshape a position and redefine your expectations.

There will also be times when you have to fire people for not doing the right thing, or because they simply weren't the correct fit for one reason or another. In my mind, that's the worst, especially when they haven't done anything egregious. I've also had to let people go when I didn't want to. There was one instance when I brought on a new partner who wanted to make our budget much leaner. I had to fire three people on the same day, which was extremely hard. We were in a place where these individuals' roles weren't needed anymore. Sadly, this happens all the time. But if your employees know that you value them and work hard for them and the company, they generally take it much better than expected.

My friend Cassandra Jones, vice president of beauty and general manager of the Ulta Beauty partnership at Target, reiterated this approach: "My best advice is to 'lead with your life,' which means to lead authentically and vulnerably and to be yourself."

Whether you run a coffee joint, a flower shop, a fashion label, or any other type of business, these are the predicaments you have to deal with. A piece of advice I would give to entrepreneurs starting their own companies is to bring on a human resources person and a management person as soon as you can. For smaller establishments, there are even virtual human resource people now. Also, take the time to compile an employee manual that outlines all your rules and policies, including days off and holidays. And make sure these rules and policies are clearly laid out from the beginning, so there's no confusion about what's expected. These are the tools that will help when issues do arise. If you want to save money, you can find human resource manuals on the internet and use them to help you formulate a guidebook that's tailored to your business's needs. Although, ultimately, you should show the final result to employment counsel to make sure your changes are sound.

The good news is that there are also very positive employer/ employee experiences when leading a company. And, over the years, I've had many of these as well. For example, my team and I took a trip to Penn State for our BOY MEETS GIRL® University initiative, which provides students with firsthand practical experience and allows us to successfully train, teach, and inform high school and college students about the ins and outs of the fashion industry (more on this in chapter 11). We had a blast preparing to partner with Rent the Runway and Campus Candy, a company that had candy stores at several college campuses. The plan was to take our runway to a candy store. It was a strong mix of people, including my employee Michelle, who worked with me for years and was instrumental in spearheading events along with other BOY MEETS GIRL® employees and interns.

We arrived at Penn State, set up a step and repeat (background banner), and were then DIYing shirts to get ready for the runway show in the candy store. It was really new and fresh, and everyone was so happy. It felt like we were all friends, even though I knew I needed to maintain some separation. This didn't mean we couldn't enjoy ourselves and have a drink to celebrate, which we did!

What's so cool is that Michelle, who ended up moving to San Francisco, wrote to me recently to say how much I taught her and that it's a big part of who she is today. She's not my employee anymore, but when I get these kinds of notes, I realize that I did something right. I'm sure there were moments when I was frustrated with her and vice versa. But we helped each other grow, and sometimes that's all you can ask for.

I always say that everyone I've worked with has led me to a different spot in my career, which has resulted in where I am today. There were certainly unpleasant moments throughout that process, but every single person has made me stronger in one way or another and shaped me into a better, more effective leader. Whether it's a licensing deal or a collaboration, you have to know how to communicate in your professional relationships and make sure that you're operating toward the same initiative to succeed.

As I said, being the boss can be a lonely prospect, even if it's exactly where you want to be. Often, you have to be your own cheerleader in order to endure.

✓ When you own a company, remember that your most committed employee will never be as committed as you are.

✓ As a boss, you can't let your employees see you sweat. You have to lead the charge by remaining poised and setting your emotions aside.

✓ It's okay to allow some give and take in the employee/employer relationship, as long as you're not a pushover.

✓ Don't make friends with the people who work for you outside the office or try to please everyone who works for you at all times; that's simply not realistic.

10

STAY CURRENT

*In order for your brand to remain relevant, you have to
change with the times and stay one step ahead of
everyone else.*

One of the most important aspects of nurturing a business
is to stay current, which was my constant focus as I was
building BOY MEETS GIRL®. Whether it was through
style and design, philanthropic endeavors, sustainability, or collaborations with up-and-coming artists, I always pursued ideas that
would disrupt the landscape of my brand in a revolutionary way,
because I wanted to make a positive impact on the world while
reaching as many people as I could in unconventional but emotionally resonant ways. With these twin goals in mind, the trends
themselves were somewhat irrelevant to me.

My focus was on reinventing the wheel by building out new
initiatives in the tech space that could reach further into our community and also make a difference through bringing awareness to
a number of different causes. So, when mastering the social media
and digital spaces became a new means of profitability in the fashion industry, I was right there at the forefront. For this reason, in
2012, I was asked to participate in Fashion 140 at Lincoln Center's

Alice Tully Hall—a one-day conference centered on social media and fashion that highlighted more than sixty presenters.

I wasn't the most self-assured public speaker on the planet at that time, but you can't allow the chaos in your mind to impede your evolution. As an entrepreneur, you have to be willing to challenge yourself and do things that are outside your comfort zone. Also, new entrepreneurs learn the hard way that, for better and worse, they are often the face of their brand. So, learning how to communicate effectively and to be comfortable in front of an audience or on camera becomes something of a requirement, especially now that the camera is ubiquitous, thanks to social media.

My friend Tracy Margolies, who first discovered me at the Workshop NY trade show in 2001 and is now the chief merchandising officer for Saks Fifth Avenue, is a firm believer that communicating with confidence is essential for business owners. She said: "When you're spearheading a team and working with internal and external partners, how you handle yourself and inspire those around you is a very important piece of who you are as a leader. I'd suggest taking classes in public speaking early on in your career."

Fortunately, I was able to set my fear aside and summon the courage to address the audience about how to humanize a brand in the digital and social media spaces. When you're growing a company, you should always be learning new and innovative things not only about your specific industry, but also how the world operates as a whole. Since I'd taken the time to do that, I was ready to educate others with the knowledge I'd absorbed through trial and error.

I discussed the Facebook page I'd created in July 2008—before fan pages were officially a thing—and how that helped generate visibility for my brand. I outlined my approach, which was to post about store events, discounts, press, and style trends. I also covered the ways in which I leveraged Twitter to highlight my business, using the handles @stacyigel and @boymeetsgirlusa. I explained that I made the conscious decision to separate my BOY MEETS GIRL® page from my personal page, so I could share what we were doing from two different perspectives. Via @stacyigel, I included behind-the-scenes moments of my life, whereas on @boymeetsgirlusa I highlighted the brand and the products. This was well before others were documenting their lives on social media. Yet somehow I knew that, even though BOY MEETS GIRL® wasn't named after me, my face still represented the human side of the business, and I wanted my customers to see that.

It brought me back to when I first launched at Bergdorf Goodman (see chapter 3) and met with the salespeople there directly, so I could train them on how to sell my product. Connecting to consumers in the digital arena was no different and was suddenly more vital than ever before. I tried to respond to every message that came to me in order to personalize the experience even further.

As I continued to foster the advancement of BOY MEETS GIRL® and work with people who were precipitating change through their art—whether it was music, sports, acting, gaming, or activism—a very cool opportunity surfaced. I met a woman named Kathy Savitt, the CEO and founder of Lockerz (now president and chief business officer at Boom Supersonic), through my web series *Behind the Seams™ with Stacy Igel*, which aired on MTVU (a digital cable television network owned by MTV Entertainment Group).

What I specifically respected about Kathy was that she was a total powerhouse and really the first woman executive I'd worked closely with on this level. She'd come from Amazon and had raised about $80 million in funding from venture capital—beyond impressive at the time. We had great synergy between us, as two women entrepreneurs. When you're exploring new industries, it's important to find strong allies who share your interests and goals.

Kathy and I formed a partnership for *Behind the Seams™* to be the only fashion-themed series to play on Lockerz, which was an international social commerce website that operated on the basis of accumulating and spending points, which members acquired by logging in, watching short videos, referring friends, answering daily questions and polls, or purchasing items. The points could then be used for discounts on clothing, electronics, fashion accessories, and other products in their shop. This collaboration was yet another means of incorporating the digital revolution into the world of clothing design. And it did really well—in fact, it was garnering the most views of all the shows on her platform.

As a result of this success, Kathy and I met in New York, and I also flew out to her headquarters in Seattle for twenty-four hours, where we took things to the next level with our partnership. We came up with the concept to allow her members to use Lockerz points to buy BOY MEETS GIRL® merchandise through the site. This was a significant development, because it was my first foray into licensing the brand online.

To continue the progress of leveraging my digital disruption, Kathy and I decided to coordinate a buy-now-wear-now show together for New York Fashion Week, which meant that people could immediately buy what they saw on the runway online. These days it's no big deal to purchase looks in real time, but back then it was unheard of. We had to build out the Lockerz site, stage a separate photo shoot with all the items, and then coordinate everything to make sure that when the pieces were being showcased, they would also pop up for sale.

I also partnered with Explore Modeling to cast my models virtually for the show, which was something designers weren't doing yet. We conducted a contest on the Explore platform where girls posted their videos from wherever they were—home, school, even parking lots.

As luck would have it, while we were planning the show, my friend Patricia Velásquez Semprún, a Venezuelan actress and model, hosted a dinner for her charity, The Wayuu Taya

Foundation, and I was seated with Wyclef Jean. Not one to pass up an opportunity like that, I asked Wyclef if he'd perform at the show in addition to up-and-comers Cris Cab and Jarina De Marco, whom I'd already recruited. I was ecstatic when he said yes and asked him to sing his version of the song "Forever Young," which we named the show after. This is proof positive that when you want something, you have to go after it, even if you think it's a long shot.

Given my mission for the brand, I wanted to give back to others with this massive New York Fashion Week undertaking and had been working with the Lower Eastside Girls Club, an organization that amplifies the inner power of young women and gender-expansive youth in New York City through their free and innovative programs in STEM, Arts, Digital Media and Sound, Wellness, Civic Engagement, and Leadership. The actress, producer, and activist Rosario Dawson, with whom I'd been friends for a few years, was on the board there, and she approached me to join forces with them. So, I came up with the idea to work with thirty of the Lower Eastside Girls Club students, roughly ages sixteen to eighteen, who'd come and shadow every aspect of what we were doing for the show. This would give them an opportunity to be part of something they wouldn't normally have access to. We assigned two girls to shadow the photographers, ten girls backstage with hair and makeup teams, and a few to be with Wyclef, Cris, and Jarina. Some of the kids helped seat the guests, others assisted the public relations team, and one tagged along with me.

I loved working with Rosario Dawson, as our missions were so aligned. Like me, she believes that "curiosity, kindness, excitement, and compassion can exist in creativity. Whatever your values are, they should be part of everything you do." Just because business is typically about turning a profit doesn't mean that there aren't other essential aspects to growing your brand.

JENNIFER FLORES

Thankfully, the show was a success on many levels. Wyclef opened by playing guitar with his tongue! And I had Olympians, musicians, top buyers, and celebrities lining the front row.

I knew it would be hard to top that. But in 2013, I made it happen by launching the biggest New York Fashion Week show of my career in partnership with Ubisoft's *Just Dance*, a multimillion-dollar, rhythm-based video game series. As a continuation of my commitment to inject modern technology into the world of fashion, I took this opportunity to conceive and create an entire collection based on a video game and then bring that vision to life.

I spent weekdays, nights, and weekends working with my team on the designs and the curation of how to infuse BOY MEETS GIRL® and *Just Dance*. For the first time, I was making party dresses with sparkles and sequins, which was unlike anything I'd done for BOY MEETS GIRL®, so it was imperative that every piece of the collection was perfect. I made a point to produce the line for the show in the heart of the Garment Center to bring everything full circle.

The plan was to use the same buy-now-wear-now formula as the Forever Young show, where the clothing we featured would be immediately available in stores and online. This meant coordinating with Ubisoft, one of the largest gaming companies in America, and distributing to the big-box retailers it was already in, like

Target. It was a turning point in my career, and I was willing to do whatever it took to make that happen.

In addition to designing and overseeing every element of the collection, I recruited celebrities with the *Just Dance* team to walk the runway, including singer-songwriter Austin Mahone, who'd just won the "Artist to Watch" Award at the MTV Video Music Awards; tennis star Sloane Stephens; and actress Brittany Snow from *Pitch Perfect*. The show was extensively covered by the *New York Times*, *Hollywood Life*, *People* magazine, *E! News*, and many other major media outlets. All eyes were on BOY MEETS GIRL® and *Just Dance*. It was a high like no other I'd ever experienced.

Unfortunately, sometimes what goes up must come down. The next week I found out that there would be no further distribution deal with *Just Dance* x BOY MEETS GIRL® into the big-box retailer chains, who simply weren't ready for a collaboration on this level yet. This was one of those times in my life and career when I had to take a moment and realize that not everything comes easily and that setbacks are par for the course, but you can still continue to move forward.

Since my digital footprint was expanding more and more with each event I participated in, I was asked to speak about all the fresh and disruptive approaches we'd taken at the FDNY Fashion Digital Conference in New York City, produced by my friend Sandy Hussain who was managing partner of OliviaPalermo.com. The day-long conference focused on ways to drive online conversions, selling product, and developing creative business strategies in fashion e-commerce. When Sandy asked me to join "The Disruptors" panel, moderated by Vanessa Friedman, who was the fashion editor of the *Financial Times* (she's currently fashion director and chief fashion critic at the *New York Times*), I couldn't say no, especially because the other panelists included Áslaug Magnúsdóttir, the CEO of Moda Operandi; David Gilboa, founder of Warby Parker; Divya Gugnani, cofounder of Send the Trend; and Nita Rollins, a futurist.

I shared all the knowledge I'd amassed about the digital space with both my colleagues and those looking to launch their own brands in the modern world of technology and social media. This included talking about my partnership with Lockerz and our buy-now-wear-now fashion show and how I'd fused my brick-and-mortar experience with Web 2.0.

It was a fulfilling moment in my career, because I truly believe that when you're an industry leader, educating others is just as important as learning everything yourself.

Today, while much of what I've done is evergreen, I'm continuing to stay current by embracing Web 3.0, which is all about community building by owning your own craft. I am leading speaking engagements with my Web 3.0 communities through my social media platforms and supporting other artists in the space. I am bridging the gap between Web 2.0 and Web 3.0 and most recently brought together twelve women in Web 3.0 for an Artist Meets Artist BOY MEETS GIRL® NFT collaboration in support of the Chicago Abortion Fund.

✓ As an entrepreneur, you have to be willing to challenge yourself and do things that are outside your comfort zone.

✓ When you're growing a company, you should always be learning new and innovative things, not only about your specific industry, but about the way the world operates on the whole and educating others at the same time.

✓ As you explore new industries, it's important to find strong allies who share your interests and goals.

✓ Even if you think something is a long shot, you have to go after it.

11

SHARE YOUR KNOWLEDGE

Always be open to learning, but sharing what you learn
is just as important, because it benefits everyone.

R ecently, someone told me that I'd make a great teacher, because I'm patient, calm, and I take time to listen to people. I credit this at least partly to the fact that I'm passionate about what I do every single day. Not once in twenty years have I gotten out of bed and said, "I can't do this," or "I don't want to do this." And sharing everything I've learned on my entrepreneurial journey allows me to maintain this passion and motivates me to keep moving.

The first piece of advice I always give budding business owners is that you have to be willing to bust your ass to succeed. When you're building a brand, there are very few stress-free days, and if you think the fashion industry—or any industry, for that matter—is all glitz and glamor, then your expectations are incorrect. Growing something from the bottom up entails endless hard work, commitment, dedication, and the ability to find the calm in the chaos when things feel overwhelming, all so that you continue to progress.

To help educate future generations, I started BOY MEETS GIRL® University in 2011. As I mentioned earlier (see chapter 9),

BOY MEETS GIRL® University was created to train, teach, and inform students—from middle school to college level—about the intricacies of the fashion field in a personalized atmosphere. We implemented various platforms such as social media, traditional marketing, campus events, and nonprofit involvement to help further demonstrate our constant engagement with our followers and offer a deeper understanding of our inclusion in the fashion tech and university spaces. Participants also gain an understanding of sourcing, sustainability, and the significance of using these methods to help a brand expand.

To achieve these goals, we've launched a number of initiatives over the last decade.

In 2013, I sent BOY MEETS GIRL® University down the runway for the first time as part of my New York Fashion Week show called "The Invasion Collections," sponsored by CONAIR STYLE 360. We did this by offering a contest with our partner Bloglovin', in which students submit a design for the show, and the selected winner would see that design appear on the catwalk, as well as be flown to New York City to attend the show and have a one-on-one dinner with me to discuss the business. This was especially cool for the younger generation, because we collaborated with singer Leah Labelle, who was represented by Epic Records in partnership with Pharrell Williams's i Am OTHER.

That same year, I worked with Lockerz again to establish scholarships for the University of Wisconsin (my alma mater), the University of Virginia, and Clemson University. I had a collaborative licensed line that was sold in the university schools' stores, and we awarded a $2,500 college scholarship to three winners we selected as the most qualified brand ambassadors. Implementing these initiatives for students and giving back was incredible and gave me a sense that I was doing exactly what I was meant to be doing. As a successful entrepreneur, it's important not only to share knowledge, but to actually assist people financially in pursuing their journey when you can.

I was also involved in Harlem's Fashion Row and the Friends of the High Line for their High Line Back-to-School Teen Fashion Show where students were paired with designers and brands such as Tabii Just, LaQuan Smith, and more. We offered the students insights into the areas of design, styling, and production, which fell under our BOY MEETS GIRL® University mission. I relished the ability to talk about my previous experiences producing fashion shows, and I let the students create their own styling vibes with a little direction from me.

My friend Tabitha St. Bernard-Jacobs—a mom, writer, artist, entrepreneur, and social impact strategist who created the Tabii Just line—offered this essential advice for the youth of today: "You have to be open to the career shifts and directions the universe sends to you, as they all hold meaning and purpose. No matter what anyone tells you, if you believe in your unshakeable faith and your own abilities, that will prevail above all else."

I'm so grateful for women like Tabitha, who know what it's like to overcome obstacles and understand the necessity of passing down their wisdom to younger generations. Stories like hers are among the many reasons I continued my mission to educate youth around the world and in various cities on topics ranging from anti-hate, anti-bullying, immigration, pride, and much more. One of those cities was my hometown of Chicago for the "When I Grow Up" event hosted by the nonprofit PJ Library, where I spoke to a hundred-plus kids, young adults, and their parents. I wrote this in my journal:

I was invited by the Jewish United Fund and PJ Library to speak this Sunday about my career to budding artists, entre-preneurs, and future designers. It was surreal. I was defi-nitely nervous inside, so when I woke up, my father and I went for a walk, got coffee, and talked. When we got to the venue, my dad was in awe of the three big screens featuring the videos we'd made at BOY MEETS GIRL® summing up the initiatives we had done. The setup was smart, and I felt great. This event was particularly special because I spoke about my Jewish upbringing and how it played a part in who I am today.

As all the kids, ages five to eighteen, filed in, I could see my dad smiling from ear to ear, and I just wanted to pause the moment. I gave my speech, which was pretty good. I'll get even better with time, but the girls, boys, and their parents were impressed. Now they all want to be designers! I guess that means it was a success. Also, the questions the students asked me were so intelligent and impressive. They wanted to know about things like manufacturing and sustainability and were truly eager to absorb everything I had to say.

I gave each one of them a very special note so they'd remember the day forever, as I know I will. I couldn't have dreamed of a better experience. It felt like a Fashion Week moment.

To me, this is what my life and career are all about—giving back, making an impact, bringing communities together, and effecting change. That's why I put together the BOY MEETS GIRL® "Live Out Loud Campaign" with Cassandra Bankson, a YouTuber who'd been bullied for her acne and whom I'd cast in several of my fashion shows. Together, Cassandra and I brought more awareness to the National School Climate Center's BullyBust program, as I'd done with Sammi Hanratty prior. Cassandra's advice for other young men and women who endure bullying is: "Surround yourself with people who understand your insecurities and support you regardless. It's okay to be nervous at times, but you have to summon the courage from within to overcome your fears. Even if you don't feel beautiful on the outside, remember that it's who you are on the inside that really matters. And if you stay true to yourself and stand up for what you believe in, the bullies will back down."

For the campaign, we asked people to use the hashtag #BMG LiveOutLoud on social media to share their "Live Out Loud" moment. The entries were everything from stories about overcoming bullying to those who'd come out as gay or transgender and even people who'd, sadly, considered suicide. It spread quickly on social media, which meant that there were tons of responses and, of course, we wanted to pick everyone. Unfortunately, we couldn't do that, but we did select one individual from each state and a few other countries, and they then filmed their narratives, which we turned into a mash-up video of their collective experiences. It was so inspirational to join forces with Cassandra in this new capacity of giving a voice to people who'd endured so much. We actually ended up inviting the winners to another fashion show that Cassandra walked in for me and, through that, we continued to create this unbelievable community of support.

COURTESY OF BOY MEETS GIRL®

These teachable moments are the fuel that keeps me going. Whether it's educating future generations about fashion or working to fight bullying, there have been so many opportunities to share the knowledge I've amassed throughout my career, which has—in turn—made BOY MEETS GIRL® a widely recognized, stronger impact brand.

> ✓ As a successful business owner, sharing knowledge with burgeoning entrepreneurs will allow you to stay grounded and motivate you to keep moving.
>
> ✓ When you're launching a brand, you have to be willing to bust your ass. Growing something from the bottom up entails endless hard work, commitment, and dedication.
>
> ✓ If you think the fashion industry—or any industry, for that matter—is all glitz and glamor, then your expectations are incorrect.
>
> ✓ It's important not only to teach others, but to financially assist people in pursuing their journey if you can.

12

COLLABORATE WITH OTHERS

Joining forces with artists, thought leaders, and brands
that inspire you will allow your business to develop in
new and interesting ways.

T hroughout my twenty-year career, I've been a big proponent of collaborating with businesses and people who
inspire me and who have a special synergy with BOY
MEETS GIRL®. Not only has it diversified our business, but it's
helped us mature and expand in unanticipated ways. Of course
there are a lot of elements that go into intertwining two different
companies, which can be challenging, but this is exactly the type
of challenge I love to embrace.

So, when Sarah Andelman, founder and former creative director
of colette in Paris, emailed a note to our sales inbox that said, "I
would love to buy your brand for my store," I was excited at the
prospect of having our clothing in such a prestigious international
boutique. I responded to Sarah immediately and said, "This is Stacy,
the founder of BOY MEETS GIRL®. If this is *the* colette in Paris, I'd
be thrilled to work with you!" colette was widely considered one of
the most important retailers in the world, featuring an eclectic mix
of toys, magazines, furniture, jewelry, and luxury men's and wom-
en's apparel, all fabulously curated by Sarah. In my opinion, there

was no more desirable launching pad internationally for a brand than colette.

Little did I know this would be the beginning of a dynamic working relationship and friendship.

Sarah ended up ordering my entire core line and, as a result of her commitment, Munir (Partner D) and I felt it was important for me to be there in person to launch the collection. So, I flew to Paris with Brian, while my mother and stepfather babysat our six-month-old son, Dylan, in New York City. I was thrilled that the recent formation with Munir on international expansion was coming together with this Parisian partnership, and I was excited to head to Paris for the meet and greet at colette. I am thankful that the launch was very successful and featured extensively by the press, which was an incredible high, until . . .

That evening, Brian and I went to an underground restaurant (with no cell service) for dinner to celebrate the event. As we were eating our meal, multiple gunmen and suicide bombers attacked a concert hall, a major sports stadium, and several restaurants and bars in and around Paris, leaving 130 people dead and hundreds more injured. We had no idea what was going on until our server told us we had to leave—everybody had to leave—because Paris was under attack. We raced back to our hotel, checking our cell phones and finding hundreds of missed calls. The first person I got in touch with was my mother who was hysterically crying after not hearing from us, since she knew that we'd been at dinner near where the attacks had occurred.

It was eerie, because everything in the city shut down and, for me, it felt like 9/11, only fourteen years later. I wrote about the experience in a piece for *LADYGUNN* magazine, which covered my journey while in Paris, and included how the following day I had a coffee in the hotel, and the man who made it for me put a heart in it. It was another of the many moments in my life when I knew I needed to find the calm in a horribly chaotic situation and remain resilient for my colleagues, my family, and my friends.

Roughly a year and a half later, with the memory of the harrowing experience in Paris in my heart, Care Bears approached me to do a collection with them. I thought it would be the perfect opportunity to work with Sarah from colette again. I suggested that we do an even bigger collaboration in Paris and, in turn, Sarah recommended Valentine's Day as the ideal date, with the theme of "spreading the love," in honor of what had happened last time I was there. She also said that they'd display the collection in their store windows as well as their water bar, which meant their whole restaurant would be branded BOY MEETS GIRL® x Care Bears x colette, down to the menus and tablecloths. We also decided to throw a party to commemorate the occasion, which was a huge achievement for BOY MEETS GIRL®.

Once the details had been confirmed, I called singer Justine Skye, who had performed in my underground New York Fashion Week show in 2015, to ask if she wanted to perform at the event, which would be her first time singing in Paris. Justine was all in and, as the day approached, the BOY MEETS GIRL® x Care Bears x colette merchandise was ready to be showcased in the windows.

Sounds simple enough, right? Not so much. As an entrepreneur, you have to be prepared for unforeseen pitfalls, and you also have to remain composed so that you can address the issue and move on.

In this case, the predicament was that one of the boxes with our unique printed collection got lost in transit, which meant we had to whip up one hundred new pieces immediately (thank you to my factory team!), because the event was being publicized in every major magazine, and I was about to fly to Paris for it.

It was absolutely nuts, but I didn't let it ruffle me. I took a deep breath and said, "I'm going to take the collection on the plane with me and no one is stopping me." I invited my father to join me, and

Nancy, my publicist for this event, and we had our other teams already on the ground in Paris along with the Care Bears team. I rolled in with my bag of clothing and saw the windows that looked incredible (and were right next to Gucci!).

Colette Roussaux, Sarah's mom and the store's namesake, who worked in the shop seven days a week, came over to me and said, "Welcome, Stacy," and then took my rolling bag from my hands and started steaming the garments. This was a milestone moment in my career, because it was from one woman business leader to another that we exchanged my pieces.

In the end, obstacles aside, the event ended up being a huge hit. There were lines around the corner and a crowd packed the store to shop the collection and watch Justine perform. The vibe was outrageous. Care Bears was happy, Justine was happy, Colette was happy, and I was happy. That to me is the sign of a magical partnership, which goes to show that even when things don't seem to be going smoothly, there's always a way to pivot.

Thanks to this collaboration, I achieved a number of my international goals for BOY MEETS GIRL® by being in one of the most renowned stores in Paris, which led to greater interest in the brand abroad. That's when Prisma, the biggest store in Finland (equivalent to Target) reached out. They wanted to license a unisex, American, woman-led brand from New York City that was making an impact for a direct-to-retailer deal. In other words, they'd have ownership of the brand in their store and country. It was a massive opportunity.

Prisma's senior vice president and director of marketing flew in from Finland and came to my office. Each side spoke about the campaigns we were working on, and they turned out to be similar in many ways. I talked about our recent launch in Paris and what we were working on in America, involving another collaboration with Macy's. Since our missions were so symbiotic, that meeting resulted in a three-year licensing deal, which eventually extended to seven years. This is why it's important to expose yourself to different kinds of partnerships. When you have an open mind and work your ass off, new possibilities often fall into your lap.

A few months later, I took a one-day whirlwind trip to Finland to meet the buying teams and sign the contract. It was truly awe-inspiring to be licensing to a hundred of their stores in Finland (and also Russia), which didn't compete with the American stores I was already in.

When the time came for us to launch the collection, I flew to Finland again for a big press event with a performance by Diandra, the Finnish pop star who was the youngest winner of Finland's singing competition *Idols* in 2012. And I gave something similar to a TED talk for the media. As the owner of a company and the face of a brand, it conveys a human element when you're present for these big opportunities, which is essential for engagement and future prospects.

The only strange thing was that when I'd finished speaking, the room was completely silent. You could literally hear a pin drop. I was like, *Oh my God, did they not understand me? What's going on?* In

America, my speeches had always been met with beaming smiles and generous applause. I was genuinely concerned I'd said the wrong thing, until one of the reporters came over to interview me after and explained: "That is our way in Finland. We don't cheer. We're very quiet." This approach was definitely surprising to me, but a learning experience nonetheless. When you collaborate with other brands, especially internationally, there are always new and interesting cultural nuances to absorb.

COURTESY OF STACY IGEL

In addition to our reciprocal business relationship with Prisma, their views on anti-bullying, cancer awareness, and sustainability were in line with everything we were doing—almost our whole collection with them was made out of recycled yarn and organic cotton—and we became the first brand to create a commercial that was filmed in America and syndicated in Finland to bring awareness to anti-bullying there. They also put billboards all over Finland, even in small rural farm areas, featuring BOY MEETS GIRL®. For nearly fifteen years of my career, I'd been dreaming that someone would invest in me in that way and that we'd have significant distribution in another country. It truly became an excellent relationship.

In 2018, I returned to Finland for the Helsinki Pride Parade, in which a million people walked. A pop-up shop was set up to sell our pride collection, including BOY MEETS GIRL®, BOY MEETS BOY®, and GIRL MEETS GIRL®, which was the first time this retailer had ever put a pride initiative in its stores that spoke to all genders, as we had been doing all along. The week was busy, coming from Paris where we launched my BOY MEETS GIRL® x Smiley "More Self Love" campaign, then landing in Finland to lead a panel surrounding pride and the initiatives I had been doing as a brand to combat hate. On top of that, I hosted a meet and greet with Finnish women and men who had driven hours to come and meet me at the textile museum at the Helsinki HAM Art Museum to discuss bullying and finding their own voices.

My licensee in Finland, Jari Simolin, senior vice president at SOK/Prisma, said, "It's necessary to partner with brands that are both authentic and well suited to your values as a company, which is why, as predicted, people truly respected the messages that our collaboration with BOY MEETS GIRL® set forth."

Of course, things were still moving and grooving back in America, where I joined forces with the Atlanta Hawks and the Chicago Bulls, my hometown NBA team. I'd partnered with Amy Serino, senior vice president of brand merchandising for the Atlanta Hawks and State Farm Arena, on a campaign to stop hate and bullying and to bring awareness to the National School Climate Center. This was the first programming with a brand like mine to lock up our logos and bring a statement.

There was a piece about our collaboration in *Women's Wear Daily* in which I'd mentioned my desire to collaborate with the Chicago

SOPHIE ELGORT

Bulls. So, by the grace of God, I was introduced to Michael Reinsdorf, the president and COO. I visited his office, met with the team, and had a pinch-me moment that I'll never forget. Everyone was on board in terms of the mission to unite our brands, and a collection was created called "Inspire With Us," through which a percentage of sales was donated to a local organization in Chicago called Center on Halsted, a lesbian, gay, bisexual, and transgender community center. As a result of this partnership, in January 2020, I was invited to speak on the Chicago Bulls court at the United Center for their Pride Night Game about BOY MEETS GIRL® and the impact we were making together. Chicago's mayor spoke as well, and I sat in the owner's box, along with Michael and Nancy Reinsdorf, Toni Kukoc, my sister, my dad, and my cousin Jackie. It truly doesn't get better than that.

The momentum kept going when I was approached by Roots, a Canadian lifestyle brand, via Nancy Lepler who was the chief merchandising officer at that time. Roots had 120 stores across North America, more than 150 internationally, and shipped to more than seventy countries via their e-commerce platform. We did a BOY MEETS

Speaking on the court at the Chicago Bulls Pride Night Game about the BOY MEETS GIRL®
x Chicago Bulls collaboration

GIRL® Roots logo mash-up and formed our Community Freedom Integrity line made out of recycled yarn and organic fabrics, which was showcased at New York Fashion Week that February of 2020.

About our partnership, Nancy said: "Collaborations result in two very different companies coming together to create something. Two very different teams and lots of opinions. In order to stay on calendar, it is essential to make approval deadlines, which can be very difficult when there are many voices that need to be heard. You have to have one person from each team spearhead initiatives and decision making. This allows for a streamlined process, clear direction, and a great product that's true to its brand DNA."

At the New York Fashion Week show, I scouted Chloe Flower, a classical pianist who had accompanied Cardi B at the Grammys, and I recruited Nycole Altchiler, one of the hip-hop dancers from another show I'd done in the past, to be the lead choreographer, which was on a much larger scale than anything she'd done before. In addition, Chloe had never had hip-hop dancers moving to her music. I also cast an eclectic group of models of different sizes, genders, and races to complete the story of harmony. To this day, it's one of the most spectacular and beautiful presentations I've produced, and it left me primed for my next adventure.

PATRICK NEREE

When you collaborate with other talented thought leaders, it inspires you to put your best foot forward and facilitates personal and professional growth.

✓ As an entrepreneur, you have to be prepared for unforeseen pitfalls so you can remain composed, address the issue, and keep moving.

✓ When you have an open mind and work hard, new possibilities often fall into your lap.

✓ Collaborating with other brands, especially internationally, will offer new and interesting cultural nuances to absorb.

✓ As the face of a brand, it conveys a human element when you're present for big opportunities, which is essential for engagement and future prospects.

13

MAINTAIN BALANCE

As a working mom, you have to find equilibrium between your personal and professional goals and commitments.

Business aside, one of my life's greatest accomplishments was becoming a mother to Dylan Reid Igel on October 4, 2014. Of course, as an entrepreneur, your career doesn't come to a screeching halt just because you're having a baby. So, even amid the chaos of new parenthood, I channeled my inner calm and forged ahead at work right up until Dylan was born.

Three weeks prior to his due date, I went in for a checkup with my doctor, who told me, "You're right on time."

Perfect, I thought. That meant I could continue to prep for a collaboration with Nordstrom, and also attend my best friend Ami's birthday party that same night, where I stayed out until one o'clock in the morning, dancing and drinking plenty of water.

Speaking of water, at 4:00 a.m., mine broke! So much for reaching my due date. Of course I didn't let that stop me from making things happen. In the midst of labor, I remembered that I was supposed to be interviewing someone for a job the next day, so I emailed her and my human resource team: "I'm on my way to the hospital to give birth. Sorry, but I have to reschedule."

When I did eventually get to interview the woman remotely, she laughed and said, "I can't believe you emailed me on the way to having a baby!" That's me in a nutshell. Nothing holds me back from pursuing my goals, even when I'm giving birth.

Thirty-three hours of labor later, Dylan was born. The minute he arrived on the scene, our world changed forever. I'd spent my whole adult life building my brand and, all of a sudden, after years of wanting to become a mom, our little family of three was complete.

Dylan did have to spend a few days in the NICU, since he'd arrived so early. Nothing is ever how they portray it in the movies. Not everyone takes their baby home immediately, and that's okay. I told myself he was going to be healthy and happy, thanks to my "Positive Polly" outlook.

Once we knew this was the case, I was up and running again on the professional front and shipping product to Nordstrom. I hadn't sold to them in a while, so when they approached me to do a collaboration and have my clothing in their stores again, I was all in.

Since Brian worked full-time and I was a newly minted working mom, we enlisted the help of a baby nurse, who stayed with us for three months. We worked in the living room side by side on our laptops at 1:00 a.m. while Dylan was sleeping, because I wanted to be as involved as much as possible without forgoing my business responsibilities. My friend Claudine DeSola, founder of Caravan, understands this plight. She said: "As a working mom, you have to learn to balance the various aspects of your life. For example, in addition to your job, you want to be a present parent and partner, if you have a significant other. It's essential to figure out how to divide your time in a way that makes sense for you and for your family."

My friend Lauren Locke, vice president of brand partnerships at Feedfeed, added to that: "My best advice is to work smarter, not harder, after having kids. This includes protecting your time by ending meetings that are no longer productive and also blocking off nonnegotiable time on your calendar to get your own stuff done."

This is one of the reasons I enlisted assistance. If you can afford it, which we could because we had spent more than a decade working our asses off, then I highly suggest it. If a baby nurse is not in your budget, having a family member come relieve some of your burden is also a great idea. My mom was with us for a month too. I always say, don't be afraid to ask for help and to accept any that might be offered.

Honestly, I don't think I took a day off. I would just work, breastfeed, hang out with Dylan, and maybe nap here or there. Since we were launching at Nordstrom the week Dylan was born, I had to deal with orchestrating everything for that, which included overseeing my team, making sure the goods were shipped promptly, and securing press coverage. It was a lot all at once. Yet, instead of going back to the office, I worked remotely every day for three months. I never took a true maternity leave as I continued to work, and I was able to be around my baby.

SPENCER KOHN

I'm not going to lie: those first three months were hard in the sense of work/mom life balance—the guilt is real on both sides, believe me. In the beginning, a lot of women were out meeting new moms, going on long walks, and talking about their day-to-day experiences. Because of my career, that wasn't something I could do.

I am thankful that Brian was a team player and a real partner. He was there with me when I was pumping breast milk and even went to the store to pick up the pump for me. What worked for us was setting up systems such as a shared Google document that tracked everything from Dylan's bowel movements to his sleep cycles. This is not to say that our methods were right or the only option. As a parent, you have to do what feels organic to you and not allow shame or culpability to overwhelm you.

I didn't have that therapeutic outlet to hash things out with other mothers until I launched my podcast, #MOMSGOTTHIS, four years after Dylan was born. I started it because I was in a working mom mindset, always on the go, building a company, and I wanted to interview other like-minded mothers who were professional rock stars in their own industries—entrepreneurs, CEOs, musicians, actors, and so on. Whether they had one, two, three children, or more, I was eager to hear their stories of how they balanced their careers with being a parent. My friend Michelle Park, who's an Emmy Award–winning broadcast journalist, TV host, and lifestyle expert, became my cohost, which was ideal because we had different perspectives, but also really respected each other's views. And she totally understood what it was like to struggle with balance and question your own aptitude. Michelle offered some wise advice for all working moms: "The biggest thing to remember is to go easy on yourself and not to fall into the mind space where you think, *I'm not good at my job, I'm not good at raising my kids,* and *I'm not being a good wife.* You have to be gentle with yourself, because there will be days when two things win and one doesn't."

Sure, there were moments when I was sad that I couldn't do all the things I saw other moms doing, but listening to these women, many of whom were in similar situations, really helped me understand that no one is perfect and that trying to handle everything yourself can be a recipe for failure. Sometimes, you have to learn to accept that doing the best you can is enough. And that it's okay to make missteps. We've all been there.

✓ Your career doesn't have to come to a screeching halt just because you're having a baby.

✓ Don't be afraid to ask for help and to accept any that might be offered.

✓ Hearing the experiences of other working mothers will alleviate your guilt and allow you to focus on the things that are important to you.

✓ No one is perfect, and trying to handle everything yourself can be a recipe for failure.

14

ROCK & ROLL WITH THE PUNCHES

When an unexpected crisis occurs, both you and your business have to pivot in order to survive.

In the last two decades as an entrepreneur, I've had plenty of unexpected challenges to overcome and hurdles to clear, and I've managed to embrace the calm throughout all that chaos. But there's been nothing as daunting as the COVID-19 pandemic and the grueling impact it had on not only BOY MEETS GIRL®, but nearly every business across the globe. For the first time in my career, I was forced to pivot my business in ways that I'd never imagined I would have to and really take stock of what was important and possible for us moving forward.

With that said, in typical BOY MEETS GIRL® style, we had one final hurrah the night before the pandemic hit on March 12, 2020. We hosted an event in collaboration with the brand Smiley, creator of the original smile (yes, someone owns the smiley face!), with whom I'd worked in 2017 in Paris. We returned to Olive & Bette's, one of the first specialty stores in New York City that carried my line early in my career. There was actually an article on the Glossy website with the headline "'The shows must go on': Why brands are moving forward with events, despite widespread coronavirus-driven cancellations" about how we'd grappled with canceling, but had decided to forge ahead with a more intimate group of fifty rather than the original 150 we'd planned for. People were definitely careful, and we took as many precautions as we could, although at that point no one was wearing masks yet, and it was still unclear what was going to happen in the coming days, weeks, and months. It was a little precarious, but—as always—I thrived on the craziness and kept my energy alive until the eleventh hour.

I had FIT students help style the windows and store as part of our BOY MEETS GIRL® University initiatives, and we dialed in remotely to dance with TikTok artist Maximo Rivano, which perhaps foreshadowed the fact that everything was about to become virtual. (Maximo had come to my New York Fashion Week show the previous month and taught me and Chloe Flower his TikTok moves on the red carpet with *Women's Wear Daily*.) There was great vitality in the air, even though life was slowly coming to a halt.

The very next day, New York City shut down—the stores, many of the restaurants, and Dylan's school. Suddenly everyone was like, *What's going on? Is this really happening? What is this going to mean for us?* Watching the news was daunting, especially for business owners. The collaborations I'd just done with the Chicago Bulls and Roots, and all the merchandise we'd produced, came to a full stop. And there was this terrifying realization that things were about to become extremely challenging, not only for my company, but for all companies. I was worried, but I knew I couldn't panic. Most important, I had to be there for my son and my family, and I also had to figure out how I was going to keep BOY MEETS GIRL® afloat. I wrote this in my journal:

#StayAtHome: Based on the recent events of the Coronavirus (COVID-19), I'm sitting here in a state of awe. I actually think we all are. I haven't had a moment to write in my journal in years. Just pieces of paper running to the subway, at the local coffee shop, or in my head while I sleep. In the past week, starting March 16, when Dylan's school became "home-schooling with mama" and the world was told to work from home, my normal—or shall I say all our normal grinds—got turned upside down. I cried and my husband hugged me. I didn't cry thinking about me, I cried thinking about my son and his normal activities and how those would come to a halt "until further notice." But because I tackle life through my glass-is-half-full motto, I have made this past week into a glorious universe filled with structure and mommy time we never would have had unless we were on vacation. I've interviewed more than sixty working moms for my podcast #MOMSGOTTHIS, and I'm certain whatever age their kids are they are feeling the same way. I definitely always envied the stay-at-home mom, as I love my time with Dylan, and while memes and funny jokes are spreading around the internet about moms drinking themselves to bed, having to take care of the kids more than they are used to, somehow I am not in that space and find it a complete joy (okay, not all the time, but you know what I mean). This week I did yoga with my son each morning, I had homeschool class with him, and taught him math, inventory management, and writing skills, and went on daily walks with him. Yet what is going to happen to my business? To me? To all of us?

I'd never been in a situation where, without warning, I was homeschooling my child (I know I was not alone in this), while work emails were spilling in from industry colleagues asking me for PPE (personal protective gear, including masks) and other medical gear for hospital employees. I felt so fortunate to be at a place in my career where, with one call or one email, I had the network to source this kind of stuff from factories. To help people in that way with the click of a button was humbling. It was like everything I'd ever done had led me to that point. And I devoted the first week of the pandemic to connecting as many dots as I could—for example, getting PPE to a hospital in Michigan through my sourcing contacts. It made me feel like I was still in control and, at the same time, so thankful that I could use my contacts to help people in need. I thought, *This is why I was put on this earth.*

Of course, I also had a lot of concerns: How was I going to pay my staff? Where would the money come from if every retail store was closed? I did have an e-commerce site and our licensees were still paying their minimum guaranteed royalties, but I wasn't sure if the people who would normally shop in person would visit our website. Or, even worse, if people actually required anything when they couldn't go anywhere. All we knew was that everyone was scrambling to stock up on toilet paper, hand sanitizer, and food. And that more and more individuals were getting sick. It was scary.

As a business owner with an international footprint, the pandemic tested the supply chain and all its stakeholders profoundly. When I spoke about this with my partner Munir, he relayed: "It was the first time that suppliers, retailers, and supply chain companies all shut down, uncertain when things would reopen. Unlike in Europe and North America, the concept of payroll protection did not exist, so a complete standstill of factories was unprecedented. Ports closed and warehouses shut down, which induced panic from workers to Wall Street. March to July 2020 were the most difficult months. As things began to open somewhat, one thing became clear—true partners and those who had boots on the ground globally were the first responders in the supply chain, sourcing the world. The negative part was the complete erosion of profitability for 2020; the positive side was that those sourcing companies that survived and stood their ground during the peak of the pandemic rebounded extremely well. In 2021, prices of raw material and freight were hiked to an unprecedented level, and this itself became a major impediment."

At the time, I had no idea what the long-term impact would be. So, as an entrepreneur and a boss, I had to be there for my employees and make sure they all felt okay, which meant reassuring them that they would still get their paychecks. And, as a parent, I had to keep things as normal as possible for Dylan, who was just five years old and my only child. It was important for me to make sure he could still play with friends in the building and meet other kids at the park. It was such a crazy, confusing time, but also beautiful in the sense that the New York community united, much in the same way it did after 9/11. I'll never forget how residents were cheering for the healthcare workers from their windows with pots and pans. Dylan joined in every night at 7:00 p.m., which gave us something to look forward to each day.

In early April, as the virus continued to spread, my sister started working for a woman named Diana Berrent, who started Survivor Corps. (She was also one of the first people in her area to test positive for COVID-19.) It began as a forum for people with symptoms and grew into an organization to connect, support, educate, motivate, and mobilize COVID-19 survivors. Three weeks after her own symptoms were resolved, she became Participant #0001 in Columbia University's clinical trial to recruit people who'd been infected with the virus to donate their blood and plasma, which was completely revolutionary.

Through my sister, Diana approached me and asked: "Can you make me masks? We need them desperately." I told her I didn't know if my factories were doing that, but I would figure out a way to make it happen, which is my MO in the midst of chaos. As it turned out, one of my factories in Canada had converted its space to manufacture PPE for hospitals, and I worked with a few of their sewers twice a week to produce the masks for Survivor Corps.

We created a pattern and got hold of as much breathable fabric and elastic as we could. I was using myself, Dylan, Brian, and my doormen as the fit models. Since Dylan was home, we decided to turn it into a project we could do together. I love how he embraced it. It really was a full circle moment for me, looking back at when I used to help my own mom. We formed a partnership with Survivor Corps to donate 50 percent of the net proceeds from the mask sales to GLAM4GOOD, an organization, community, and movement that "ignites positive social change through style." Right away, we raised two thousand dollars for it.

The press ended up covering these efforts and the fact that BOY MEETS GIRL® was one of the first brands to create masks, which was how we were able to sustain and grow our e-commerce site. It was a major pivot for me and my company, but it also kept the lights on and allowed us to continue doing impactful collaborations that made a difference. In addition to Survivor Corps and GLAM-4GOOD, those collaborations included WellEgan to fight racism (for Black Lives Matter and George Floyd), Annabel Daou for Impact Lebanon, Fashion Our Future 2020 (to support their mission based on our previous work with Voto Latino and Youth Empower, encouraging youth to register and vote), and a Holiday Market curated by Dylan and me to help other entrepreneurs, creators, and nonprofits.

I was doing what I do best, which was joining forces, collaborating, and raising awareness, in the midst of so many horrible things going on in the world. And, on the home front, I was undertaking more than ever before—like teaching a kindergartner and cooking every meal. (I was also eating a lot of chocolate-covered almonds and making long overdue use of my Netflix subscription.) While Brian pitched in where he could, like most moms out there, I had essentially no homeschooling help.

Still, if not for the pandemic, Dylan would never have had the chance to immerse himself in my daily grind. After observing some of my efforts to give back, he and his friend Noa set up a lemonade stand outside our local coffee shop. They combined their names to call it DOA and crafted handmade signs. All the neighborhood kids came, and a percentage of their sales was donated to No Kid Hungry.

In many ways, even though it should have been a stressful time (which it was at moments), being at home really took me back to the very beginning, when I was designing clothing in my bedroom.

In July 2020, after having an office in the Garment Center for more than fifteen years, my lease was up. My whole team met for the first time since the pandemic hit. We came together and packed everything up so we could enter the brave new world of working remotely.

In the end, while this period definitely changed the way I viewed my business in many ways, it didn't change the way I lead my life as an entrepreneur. As my friend Sarah Clagett, who's a producer at the *Today* show, said, "You have to make sure you're always striving for something in your journey, even though you may not know what it is in that moment."

Life is a marathon, not a sprint. You have to focus on what's in front of you and remain in your own lane, at least most of the time. It's taken me a while to recognize that "success" comes in many forms. There are people who started out when I did who are now billionaires and there are also people who are no longer in business. My business is somewhere in between, but much more important, I feel wildly successful as a human being. I'm excited to go to work every day, which is now in my home again, in the park, out in Secaucus, New Jersey, and anywhere else in between. I love the people in my orbit, and I have an outlet to do the things that make me feel good about myself and the world I will leave behind for my son. I feel pretty freakin' rich, to be honest, and I'm completely content with where I am as a business leader and as a mother. I also know that the future holds an incredible number of exciting opportunities for BOY MEETS GIRL®—more partnerships, collaborations, endless licensing, and giving back to communities in need.

That's why I wrote this book—so that up-and-coming entrepreneurs and even those who currently own companies understand it's not just about raising millions of dollars from investors. You can make money, you can give back, you can work with unbelievable thought leaders and still be there for your family.

You just have to tune out the noise. Be true to yourself. Keep moving . . . at your own pace.

And, as always, *embrace the calm in the chaos*!

APPENDIX

In the introduction to this book, I explained that throughout the last twenty years of building my brand, I've learned so much from my friends and colleagues—a group of exceptionally talented and ambitious entrepreneurs and leaders with whom I have authentic connections. You've already heard some of their expert advice, and now it's my great honor to share these sixteen rousing interviews, which provide deeper insight into how to achieve success while maintaining balance and sanity. It's my hope that you'll learn as much from these gifted individuals as I have, and that their words of wisdom will inspire you to keep moving forward in your journey.

Sophie Elgort

PHOTOGRAPHER, DIRECTOR, ARTIST

Over the past decade, you and I collaborated on more than fifteen campaigns. However, you were premed in college. What inspired the transition?

I think a lot of people follow in their family's career footsteps, because they grew up around it and it's what they know. Others have the mindset to rebel. They don't want to do this thing that everybody expects them to do. During college, I was actively looking for what my thing was going to be. I did lots of different internships. I was also in an a cappella group and, ironically, everyone in it was premed. I remember struggling with what I wanted to be, so I decided to do all the premed requirements, in case I decided to go that route. Once I graduated and was back in New York City, ensconced in the creative world again, I realized that being a doctor was not for me.

I applied to a few jobs on Craigslist and got two of them. One was to be an intern at the Peggy Siegal Company; she does film publicity. The other one was to work on the team for this new nightclub concept that hadn't even opened yet. They had just found the space, and they needed someone to help them launch. I took both jobs, since the nightclub was paying and the Peggy Siegal Company was an internship. I was the first person hired to work for the nightclub, and it was all encompassing, so when they ended up opening I got to pick whatever position I wanted. I was twenty-two years old, and I thought marketing director sounded like a great title. I didn't even know what that meant, but there it was on my business card.

At the same time, my friends were launching a repurposed vintage e-commerce site, and they needed photography, which I was always doing as a hobby. They asked me who to hire and I had no idea. Then they said, "What if you do it for us in exchange for clothing?" That sounded like a great deal to me. So, I started shooting their collections, and the pictures got picked up by MTV, *Teen Vogue*, and lots of other media outlets. As a result of that, more photography work began rolling in, and I basically built a portfolio by accident. It was right when social media was becoming a big thing, and I never looked back.

Did growing up behind the lens with your father—Arthur Elgort—inspire or shape your career choice?

I spent a lot of my childhood on set. My mom is a director, so I grew up on and in her productions. I would also go with my dad to his studio and travel with him on shoots. Often, it was my after-school activity, so I feel like I've been learning photography and directing my whole life without even thinking about it. I had an awareness of the photo shoot process from the time I was really young, which made it comfortable and natural to me.

I don't know if I would say I wanted to be a photographer back then, but from the time I was a young kid, I would dress up, style, and take pictures of my friends. Then I'd get the film developed and hand out the photos at school. So, even though I may not have been sure I wanted to pursue it long term, it was definitely something I was exposed to through my father.

In my family, we have a very competitive spirit and a go-getter attitude. Did your mom and dad shape your work ethic in the same way?

Definitely. My family instilled a good work ethic in me from an early age. No matter what I was doing, they wanted me to be passionate about it and committed. Though they never pushed me toward one thing or another, I was held to what I chose to pursue. If I said I wanted to be on the swim team, I had to go to every single practice. I remember one time, growing up, I went to a sleepover with a bunch of friends and we were up super late that night. I had practice the next morning, a Saturday, at 6:00 a.m., and I called my mom to tell her I was too tired to go. She said, "Sorry, that's not a good excuse; you're going." That's how I was raised.

We've always talked about finding new artists who are shining lights. For example, in 2015, we shot model Lameka Fox on her first job. What is that discovery process like for you?

One of the things that's always been exciting and interesting to me about you is that you have the guts to try things before other people are doing them. That's part of why I love collaborating with you, because you're not afraid to take that leap. I love finding talented people as they're coming up. I think when you meet them in person, you can often tell if they're going to be a star. It's not just how somebody looks; it's their personality and how they carry themselves. It's also about giving them a chance. That's something that I learned from my dad at an early age, since he discovered a lot of the big super models and gave them their first chances.

He told me a story about when he wanted to photograph Christy Turlington, before anyone knew who she was and nobody had shot her yet. He called the modeling agency she was with and said, "I'd like to shoot this girl."

They said, "Okay, but we have much better girls."

And he said, "Well, she's the one I want." He saw something special in her and gave her the chance. After that, she blew up. The point is, there are plenty of people out there who have the potential to be stars, but somebody has to see that potential and give them the exposure to fulfill it.

At my New York Fashion Week show in 2012 with Wyclef Jean, Cris Cab, and Jarina De Marco, we collaborated to capture street style live. We had to create these things together before social media existed as it does today. Can you talk about that?

You were always trying new things that could make your collections into an experience, and I admired that. I was taking pictures for you, and we were uploading them live to Tumblr—we figured out how to sync it so that my camera uploaded them as I was shooting. It was cool we did that, because a few years later people and publications started documenting shows live via Instagram, and now of course people stream their shows live. It was really the beginning of that.

What would you teach a budding photographer about perseverance?

I think a lot of artists are full of self-doubt and suffer from imposter syndrome, which is when you question your own accomplishments and accolades. I'm always relieved when I hear major creatives who talk about this—it's refreshing to know you're not the only one who feels this way. I think the way to get past it is to keep making work; creating. The road to where you want to go is not always linear; you have to keep trying various paths. You learn to not take no for an answer. You have to have perseverance.

During the pandemic, you did an interview series with your father. Can you share what it's about?

Yes, it's called "Behind the Lens with Arthur Elgort." It came about because, for a big part of quarantine, my family was isolating together, and we were living in my parents' house for months. My dad and I started having conversations about his career and work, some stories that I only knew portions of and others I didn't know at all. So, I decided to start recording our conversations and center each one around a different picture or set of pictures. He would tell me the story behind an image, and I would ask questions along the way. Each interview was about ten minutes long, and it was a really organic process.

Through these stories, I learned a lot about his career and, also, my dad as a person—his drive and dedication, his genuine interest in people. It was inspiring. We would literally set an iPhone down anywhere and just talk. It wasn't produced, and I barely even edited it. It turned into something really special, and we had a lot of fun with it. That's my style. I like things that are real, especially in this day and age when often the only things shown are highly edited and unrealistic. The most positive feedback I received about the series was that it was so authentic. I'm proud of what we did. And, above all, we really enjoyed spending the time together.

You have a daughter, Stella, and a son, Artie. Do you take them on set with you?

I loved doing that growing up, so I would definitely like to do a similar thing with my kids. Artie is still a baby, and—because of the pandemic—Stella hasn't been on set with me in a year and a half, but moving forward I want to keep the tradition alive. I think it's a gift to be able to work and also have your family around.

Ike Barinholtz

ACTOR, WRITER, PRODUCER, DIRECTOR

We've been best friends since we were in preschool. Back then, did you know you would become a star?

Well, when I was a baby, a young gypsy woman put her hand on my head and said, "You will be a star." No, I'm kidding. Early on, I actually wanted to be a politician. My dad was friendly with some guys who were involved in local Chicago politics, and I was very enamored with it. It seemed like a job where you could help people, but it also seemed fun, and there was always really good food around. I mean, I took it seriously enough that, in high school, I didn't smoke weed because we were still living in the Bill Clinton era, and he had all this stress when he lied about it. If you recall, our families went on a vacation to Jamaica together when we were sixteen, and all of these cool tourists and local Jamaicans were smoking huge joints, and I said: "None of that for me. I'm going to be president one day." It was literally the lamest possible thing anyone could have said. What a loser!

Still, I really was interested in going down that track for a while. But I also loved movies and TV shows. Growing up, the thing I did more than anything was watch movies. If you ask me any movie trivia question, I'll probably be able to answer it. But I often forget where I parked my car. So, it's not like we're dealing with something like *A Beautiful Mind* here. Anyway, when I was in college, I started feeling like politics might not be my thing, and it began crystallizing in my head that I wanted to write a movie and star in it one day.

Then I got kicked out of college, and I knew I wanted to do something with acting, but I didn't know what it was until I saw the Improv Show in Chicago and was so blown away by it. I really just launched myself into that.

I'm guessing acting didn't pay the bills in the beginning. How did you deal with that?

That is correct. When I got kicked out of school, my parents were like, *Just so we're clear, you will be getting a job that pays you money.* And improv doesn't really do that. So, I had a day job at the Chicago Transit Authority (CTA) and would take improv classes at night. After that, I took a job at The Second City, an improv comedy club in Chicago, and I learned a ton there just by watching sketches in between cleaning up vomit and garbage. It was a really great time to be there. I got to watch Tina Fey, Rachel Dratch, Horatio Sanz, Kevin Dorff, Scott Adsit, and all of these amazing performers, which made me fall in love with it more and more. After training for six months or so, I had the chance to perform. I remember a bunch of friends coming to my early shows and being really bummed out because I'd worked so hard but wasn't that great. But I kept performing, and after a while I started getting comfortable in my skin. By the time I left Chicago, I was doing five to seven shows a week, and I was much better. There's nothing like having your close friends come see you do well and laugh.

Did the jobs at CTA and The Second City shape who you are today?

Definitely. You have to have a roof over your head and be able to eat. It's important that people understand that whatever your dream is, whether it's fashion, writing, stand-up, or anything else, it's okay to have a job that's not necessarily tied into that. You have to look at it as a means to an end, as in, *I need this money to pay rent.* And you should never be ashamed of that. Just because you have a day job as a waiter doesn't mean you're not a writer, as long as you're writing and working toward your real goals. Take whatever job you can that will pay you enough, even if it sucks. Don't let it inhibit your development of what you think you were put here to do.

Growing up, your mom used to give you books and notes of encouragement, as did my dad. Were your parents always supportive of you, even during hard times?

My parents have been the most supportive people throughout my life and have always motivated my creativity. My mom was very into the author Joseph Campbell, who wrote *The Hero with a Thousand Faces*, which talked about the broad strokes of the hero's journey. So, I read a lot, which they nurtured. When I told them I wasn't going to finish college, they were definitely annoyed, but once they saw that I was pursuing my passion, they came around and were at every one of my improv shows. There was actually one night when the only paying customer was my dad. So, yes, they've always been there for me, which sometimes meant giving me an honest critique. And I'd be like, "Shut up, that's not what I'm paying you for." I'm joking. I'm not paying them anything, unfortunately. But they are the greatest.

In early 2001, I flew out to Los Angeles, and we drove to Fred Segal, along with your good friend Seth Meyers, so I could show them my samples. And I made a sale! Do you remember that?

I remember that trip like it was yesterday, because it was so consequential for my friends and for me. You always knew what you were put on this earth to do, and you were so focused on it. You were one of my first friends to find success in your field. You were like, "We're going to Fred Segal, and I'm going to sell them my clothing." When you came outside and said you'd done it, I was so excited, because we were young kids and you were making something of yourself.

We went out to dinner that night to celebrate, and Seth Meyers, who had auditioned for *Saturday Night Live* a week or two before, found out he was getting hired. It was so amazing that both of those things happened on the same day. Even though I was still trying to be a busboy at a restaurant, I was fine with it. I was blown away that two of my friends were off and running.

From that point on, what was the trajectory of your career? Were there a lot of highs and lows?

Yes, there were a lot of highs and lows. I was working at a restaurant, starting to get a little frustrated that I couldn't catch a break, and then a miracle happened. I did a two-man sketch show with Seth Meyers's brother, Josh, that we wrote. We asked all of our friends to come, and my friend who'd been on MADtv knew that a bunch of cast members were leaving. She saw the show and then got one of the MADtv producers to come. Because of that, we landed an audition and were hired. That was a big step for me and what I consider the beginning of my career. I was there for five years and had a great time. But, even though I was working and getting paid pretty well, I wanted more.

At the tail end of my time there, I met my wife, Erica. The show was on its last legs, and they didn't have enough money to keep me. I remember thinking, *Oh shit, my girlfriend just moved out to L.A. and now I don't have a job.* After that, I had a really difficult three and a half years where I wasn't getting cast in much. I was doing some silly spoof movies, which I was super grateful for, because they paid. One of them gave me money to buy Erica an engagement ring, which was nice, but it was still so far from what I wanted to be doing. I realized that I wasn't getting hired as an actor, so I had to commit to writing. My buddy Dave Stassen and I partnered up and started writing movies together. We sold the second or third one we wrote, which was *Central Intelligence*. That was the first time where I said to myself, *I just sold a screenplay to a movie studio; I can exist in this space.*

How did you keep moving? Did you say, *I'm unstoppable* all the time?

I wouldn't say I felt unstoppable all the time. During pilot season, there's this horrible process where you audition, and if the casting director likes you, they bring you in front of producers. If the producers like you, they bring you into the studio. If the studio likes you, you go to the network. If the network likes you, you get the part. It's called testing. And I tested for twenty to thirty shows over the years. It was this perpetual cycle of auditioning for shows I didn't even like, but I knew would pay me good money. I'd convince myself that playing the wacky neighbor on some show was going to be so great, and then I wouldn't get the part, which was a real bummer. But I kept pushing and pushing. And I'm glad I did because there was one day when I got a call about a show called *Eastbound & Down*. I'd been a huge fan of the first two seasons—it was probably my favorite show on TV. I was on my way in to audition for a part, and they called me to say the part was no longer available.

I said, "Is there anything else?"

They told me there was an opening for a Russian character.

I said, "I'll do it; I can do a Russian accent." I went in and auditioned with the star of the show, Danny McBride, and I eventually got cast.

That role got me back in the game. Mindy Kaling ended up tweeting that I was really funny, and we started following each other. From there, Dave Stassen and I met with her to be writers on *The Mindy Project*, before it went to air, and we were hired to do that for six seasons. It was and still is the best job I ever had. It really helped people hear my voice.

Do you have advice for aspiring actors?

I get asked this a lot, and it's weird. I used to be able to give the standard answer, which I believed, which was to sign up for Upright Citizens Brigade or any kind of improv within a hundred miles of you. But everything's changed. A lot of those places are gone. So, now I'd say you have to figure out exactly what you want to do and put yourself out there, especially online, like YouTube or on other social media sites. Seth Meyers just hired a guy who's a writer and performer because he made really funny little Twitter videos. People have access to a lot of tools that I didn't back in the day.

Aside from putting yourself out there, the other advice I would give, and this applies to any field, is that you have to find what you really love and then think about it and work on it every day. Even if you're on vacation with family, it should be in the back of your mind, and there should be nothing stopping you from taking five minutes here or there to invest in it. Of course you want to be able to turn your brain off, but at some point in the day you want to think about what you're doing, what you want to do, what your next thing is, and what the next story you want to tell is. If you're truly passionate about something, it will be all-consuming.

In addition to having a successful career, you're also a father of three. What does the future hold for you?

For the last few years, I've been doing what I moved to Los Angeles for, which is making movies. I just wrote and directed a movie and wrote and starred in another one that Dave directed, which is our goal. That, along with some fun acting gigs here and there, is what I've been doing, which is great. There's definitely been a part of me that was like, *God, I want to do a TV show.* So, we're about to start doing one, which we're very excited about. Professionally, I feel super blessed and happy with where I am right now.

I also have three little girls who mean the world to me, and I really try to balance my home/work lives so I can be present for them as often as possible. In other words, I'm probably not going to go do a movie if it means I have to spend six months in New Zealand. I'm never going to be away from them for that long. People have different balances, which is fine, but I get a little crazy if I don't get to see my family a lot. I'm very lucky that my wife understands the business enough that if I run into my office mid-sentence to send myself a quick email, she doesn't think it's weird. I know how fortunate I am to have a team—and by team, I mean family—who's continuing my parents' tradition of supporting me blindly.

Tracy Margolies

CHIEF MERCHANDISING OFFICER, SAKS FIFTH AVENUE

In all my years of knowing you, I've never dived into how you started your career path. Was fashion always in the cards for you?

I grew up around fashion and retail. My grandmother and my great-aunt owned a dress store with an accessories boutique in Brooklyn. As a child, I would go in on the weekends and help my grandmother organize the handbags or I'd go with her to trade shows at the Javits Center. So, from an early age, I had a love for retail.

I pursued a degree in psychology at the University of Maryland, because I always wanted to help people and that field always interested me. However, I eventually realized that I likely wouldn't be able to separate my feelings from the job, and it wouldn't be the best career path for me. Thinking about my love for retail, I realized my expertise in psychology would help me better understand how people shop and express themselves through their personal style. From then on, I decided that I wanted to pursue the business side of fashion.

I took an internship at Bloomingdale's when I was in college, under the premise of the psychology of retail, which taught me a lot. After graduating, I took another internship at Bergdorf Goodman and spent the first ten years of my career on its buying team. I joined Saks as the vice president and divisional merchandise manager of women's footwear and then went back to Bergdorf Goodman for several years as a senior vice president and general merchandise manager across multiple divisions. I ultimately returned to Saks as the chief merchant, where I led the merchandising strategy for the company. All in all, I knew that I wanted to be a buyer, because it requires both a creative and business mindset, and I could use both sides of my brain. The energy of fashion and retail combined was exactly what I was looking for in my career.

It's hard to believe that we met twenty years ago at the Workshop NY trade show, which was my first show in New York City. You helped put my brand on the map, which was a huge moment for me. When you discover a brand, do you get the same adrenaline that a designer gets? And do you think about the long-term trajectory of that brand?

Absolutely. I love to support and encourage young designers who are just starting out and who like to take chances. As the chief merchant of a luxury retailer, I have the ability to make an impact on a designer's career, and I want to do whatever I can to help them. I'm always thinking about how to expand relationships with emerging designers and help them achieve mid- and long-range plans to grow their brand.

As a working mom myself, I'm interested in hearing about the journey of other working moms. You chose to become a single mother later in life. How do you balance career and parenting on your own?

I've always said that I wanted a work-life balance. It is critical to my success to figure out how to be 100 percent present, no matter what I'm doing—whether it's personal or professional. My son is only four right now, but one thing we've done since he was a baby is participate in photo shoots for Saks, as well as Mother's Day photo shoots at home. It's a wonderful experience to see how much he's grown through this lens. He loves to be around people, so he eats it up! It's a fun tradition we have together, and it reveals my personal side to Saks clients and my colleagues. As a leader in the industry, I think it's important to show the full perspective—that women can be successful in their careers and as mothers.

Do you have insight or advice for other budding entrepreneurs who are looking to have children?

If I'd asked my younger self whether I'd have children sooner or later, I wouldn't have guessed that I'd wait until I was in my forties. That being said, this is where I am. My journey was such that I was going to either have a child late in the game, or not have one at all. I remember a friend said to me, "You'll only have regrets if you don't do it." And she was absolutely right. Having a child was the best decision I've ever made in my entire life. The joy that my son brings me is unparalleled, and the love that I have for him is above and beyond anything I ever expected. I have a great peer group of mom friends, and we all count on each other. I also have a great network of other friends and family. I think that kind of support is essential.

What's something important that you did in your career that had a real impact on your success?

It's really important to learn from as many different people as you can, in as many different areas of the business as possible. Whether they're good managers or bad managers, you absorb something from everyone. When you expose yourself to different categories within your field, the benefit is a wider strategic mindset, which helps you become a stronger merchant. My goal was always to build a career rather than just have a job. Those two things are completely different. When you pursue a career, there's emotion and passion involved. When I'm in the process of growing my team, those are the kinds of people I look for, because you can teach skills, but you can't teach passion; that's irreplaceable.

What's been the hardest challenge in your career?

In a business like fashion, it's never nine to five. There are important things that occur after work hours, like events and social activities, that you want to be a part of. Sometimes when I can't attend something, I feel guilty about it. Or, when I'm traveling too much, I feel guilty about that. I want to be everywhere, but I also want to be home. You have to find the right balance for you.

Can you share a story where you really had to push yourself to achieve your goal at a high-stakes moment in your career?

When we were thinking about expanding the shoe salon at Saks Fifth Avenue, we came up with the idea to move the entire department from the fourth floor to the eighth floor to allow for more space. I was worried that customer traffic wouldn't make it up there, so I assembled an internal team to collaborate and brainstorm ways to generate excitement around visiting the new shoe floor. We created a shoe department so big, the U.S. Postal Service granted the floor its own zip code—and that's how we came up with the name 10022-SHOE. It quickly became an iconic part of the store that was well known, not only throughout the city and the industry, but around the world. We also saw other stores emulate what we did, which was even more gratifying. This was a proud moment in my career when I took a challenge and, with the help of my team, created something spectacular.

What's one piece of advice you can give to women on being successful in the fashion industry and/or starting a business in fashion that is surprising or unexpected?

One of the best pieces of advice I can offer to women in business— fashion or otherwise—is to communicate with confidence. If I had the opportunity to guide my younger self, I'd suggest taking a lot more public-speaking classes. As you're spearheading a team and working with internal and external partners, how you present yourself and inspire those around you is a very important piece of who you are as a leader. I've always prided myself on being extremely honest and genuine, but I wasn't always as outgoing as I am today. I was the one in the back of the room, speaking when spoken to. Cultivating self-assurance, especially in front of a large crowd, is something I continue to work on to this day.

Dana Pollack

CEO AND FOUNDER, DANA'S BAKERY

We met many years ago at an event for a mom group called HeyMama in New York City and connected as two women entrepreneurs. When did you decide to pursue a career in the food industry?

I wasn't always a pastry chef, and I definitely wasn't a business owner. I actually went to school for photography and worked in the photo editorial world for more than ten years. The last job that I had before I made my life change was as photo editor for *Muscle & Fitness* magazine.

I was sitting at my cubicle, just about to turn thirty, and I was staring at this photo of a man in a Speedo from one of my photo shoots. I was like, *Am I really going to be doing this for the rest of my life? Where do I see myself in five to ten years?* I would look at the people who were above me in the company and think, *I don't know if I want that for my life. Something needs to change.* I said to myself, *Let me just bring it back to basics. What do I love doing? What makes me happy?*

I realized pretty quickly that I've always been the person who bakes to alleviate stress, and if I was ever trying to impress someone or show someone that I cared, I would bake for them. I love to entertain and get creative and think outside the box with recipes. It's been my thing since I grew up baking with my grandmas. I have a huge sweet tooth! So I thought maybe there was something I could do with that, but I didn't really know what it was. Instead of quitting my job to bake cakes out of my tiny New York City apartment, I decided to get formal training and found the Institute of

Culinary Education in New York City. Within a week or two, I gave notice at my job, and I started the next phase of my life.

Were you working while you were in culinary school, and did you know at that point that you were going to start your own business?

Yes! I was hustling and always burning the candle at both ends. When I was in school, which is a full-time job in and of itself, I was also working at restaurants to gain experience with everything from prepping to production, often until one o'clock in the morning. During that time, I met my now husband, and I'm pretty sure he was like, "Who is this thirty-year-old chick who's back in school?" But he loved and respected my drive. You need a partner who's going to support you in that way, because when you start your own business, it's a lot of freaking work.

Though I will say that I didn't know that I was going to become an entrepreneur immediately. I was so immersed in learning new skills and the history behind it all. I'm actually a trained pastry chef, and there are so many things you can do with that. You can become a caterer, you can work at a restaurant, or you can start your own venture. Through my experiences, I realized that restaurant life was not for me. And, midway through school, I fell in love with French macarons. I kept seeing the same French flavors, like lavender, rose, and pistachio, everywhere. I didn't understand it; we were living in America! Where were the red velvet and the s'mores? I became totally focused on creating the anti-macaron—the punk rock version— which is very much my MO with everything. That's how the concept of Dana's Bakery was born, and it took off from there.

What did launching your own business look like for you?

I started developing the concept and new recipes toward the end of my culinary school training. I didn't have any partners, and I still don't. I also didn't have any investors at the time. I was hesitant to start with a retail location, because rent in New York City is absolutely insane. I always tell burgeoning entrepreneurs that you don't necessarily need a brick-and-mortar location; it's really dependent on what you're selling.

At the time, we were the first exclusively online bakery. I had a friend who built my website. I knew how to do all the photography, and the overhead was a lot cheaper to have a commissary kitchen that I could rent a couple of hours a week to develop and make these recipes. This way, we didn't have to invest in all the equipment, just my ingredients and my labor. Customers would order online and I would hand deliver to them in New York City, where I lived. Then, through social media, the word spread, and we started to get demand from other states. That was when I had to figure out the logistics and cost of shipping, which meant I had to hire more employees. I put everything I made back into the company to help it grow. It was a very natural evolution.

Do you wish you'd had financing in the beginning?

No, because I know more now than I did then, and I probably would've given away too much and "gone to bed" with the wrong partner. I've met a lot of slithery snakes along the way. Maybe I didn't get all of that capital as early, but I got there eventually, and now I'm at the point where I'm confident in the business. I know where it needs to go, and I can hire the right people so that we can get from Point C to Point Z in the proper way. I've made mistakes, but I'm definitely happy that I didn't take outside financing in the beginning, because I wasn't educated enough or comfortable enough within the business to be able to make the correct decisions.

What were some of your struggles with running Dana's Bakery?

Everything was a struggle! I didn't go to business school, so I didn't know my ass from my elbow, but I had to figure it out. My mom helped me create my LLC with a family lawyer. I would even ask people in the commissary kitchen to help me understand my costs. I lost so much money in the beginning. I spent more paying for taxis to deliver my food than what I was actually making by selling it. There was a lot of waste, and there were many lessons learned.

There were also plenty of times when I was going about making something a certain way and it was just taking us too long, or when I hired the wrong people. I once ordered the incorrect packaging without testing it, and I had thousands of dollars of packaging that I couldn't use because customers' orders were arriving broken.

I would say that the first two years of any new business, regardless of whether you went to business school or not, are a major learning curve, because you have no data to pull from. You just hope and pray you'll stay afloat. Luckily, I think that because of my marketing, my social media, my photos, and because I had a really good product, I hit the wave at the right time. We were profitable from year one. Not super profitable, but profitable, and then it was about growing.

The grind is so real in the beginning. You have a lot of highs and just as many lows.

What advice would you offer to someone starting out as an entrepreneur in any field?

I find that a lot of people are very intimidated to start a business, so they focus on things that will prevent them from actually starting, a.k.a. their business plan. People spend so much time working on the business plan that they're not actually working on their business. They almost use it as a scapegoat to avoid actually getting into the nitty-gritty. Listen, you definitely need to have some type of outline, some type of goal, and some benchmarks that you want to hit in the near and far future. However, if you spend a year or two working on a business plan, as soon as it's done, you're going to have to update it, which makes no sense.

Instead, figure out the first five things that you need to accomplish. What do you need to get your business up and running? Check off those things, and then start to outline the next five. I find that people make so many excuses out of fear.

You have to keep moving and be passionate about what you're doing. If you own your own business and you're not 120,000 percent into it, you'll give up. It's every second of every day. It's knocking on doors, it's nights, it's weekends. It's all-consuming. It's that kind of dedication.

Cassandra Jones

VICE PRESIDENT, GENERAL MANAGER, BEAUTY AND
ULTA BEAUTY PARTNERSHIP AT TARGET

**We met when we did a collaboration with Macy's and immediately
realized that we're both Midwest girls who built our names from the
ground up. Have fashion, retail, and beauty always been your calling?**

If they were, I wouldn't say I knew that when I was growing up in
the Midwest. I was coached by my parents that success meant
becoming a doctor or a lawyer. Of course, this was before social
media, when there were no more than twenty channels on the TV.
Yet, I had this global perspective and interest in humanity, because
we had about twelve foreign exchange students in the eighteen years
that I lived with my parents. And I remember them bringing in
international magazines and wearing clothing that I'd never seen.
As a result, I started creating these massive collages about fashion
and art.

When I got to college, I actually became a finance major, and
my first role was balancing trades for a trading company. After four
or five months, I listened to my inner voice, which told me that
what I was doing wasn't making me happy. I figured I would end
up going to law school, but then I thought long and hard and said
to myself, *What do you love to do?* And the answer was, shop at the
mall. I'm not joking. So, I decided I needed to work at a retail company, and I began my journey by getting a job at Dayton-Hudson
Marshall Field's. It was the first time I was doing something that

appealed to my creative side, even though I couldn't necessarily articulate that.

Did you follow a traditional career path to get where you are today?

No, I don't think there is a traditional career path. I was in retail for a few years in my twenties and still trying to figure out who I was and what to do with my life. I took my LSAT (heeding my parents' advice), but I really wanted to find a way to give back to humanity. So, I quit my job, sold everything, and went to serve in the Peace Corps in Nicaragua, where I taught small business skills. Through that experience, I started to realize who I was as a person and how I could have an impact on the world.

After the Peace Corps, I returned to work in retail for Midwest department stores and did sourcing for a few years. Then, once again, I realized I wanted more, so I sold everything and moved to a three-hundred-square-foot apartment in New York City. I took a chance on myself and landed a role at Macy's, which launched the trajectory of my leadership journey. I had several different roles there, both within merchandising and outside of merchandising, that ultimately led me to be the senior vice president of fashion and digital strategy, which is where you and I connected for the first time.

While I learned a lot during my tenure at Macy's, I knew that wasn't the end-all for me. I wanted to be a part of a company that was helping create the future of retail, and I also wanted to generate diversity and inclusion in the boardroom. I thought, *If I'm being asked to simulate a white male leadership style and I'm a skinny white girl, how are we ever going to effect change?* I wanted to work somewhere that allowed me to lead authentically and vulnerably and, also, a place that would let me shift the traditional operating system of leadership. This led me to move across the country, where I joined the ranks at Target.

You mentioned that you've moved multiple times. How has that impacted your family life?

I've been relocating since I was a child. My family moved six times before I was seven years old, and I've continued that into adulthood. I'm always open to the possibility of experiences and building a community wherever I land. I look at it as a way to grow as a person. I'm now married and have two kids, so when we move, we have to approach it as a partnership. We ask ourselves: *How are we going to do this together? What's going to happen to each of us on this journey? And are we all equally open to being flexible with one another in order to figure out how to tackle this new lifestyle?* There's definitely culture shock when you move a family from New York to the Midwest, and you have to be honest with one another about when you're having a great day and when you're not. You have to, collectively, figure out the new norms and then actively build a community around you to make sure that you have enough people to fill you up.

The fashion and beauty industries are constantly transforming. How do you think your experiences and knowledge have influenced your current job at Target?

I've always thought that my purpose in the merchandising area of retail is to sell experiences and emotions. When you buy a new shirt or your favorite color lipstick, it's because it makes you feel something, whether that's preparedness for a first date or a job interview or just as a pick-me-up. I believe that my ability to adapt and change has made me very aware of people's different needs, and how to think about what I now call "the guess"—the central factor in all of the decisions that I make.

The more experiences you have, the easier it is to see the things behind you and the things ahead of you, but also to accept that you might not know all of those things. You have to surround yourself with others who can help you react to whatever's happening in a business, in an economy, and in a community so that you're primed as a team to ebb and flow with the changes of the industry.

Do you have a personal mantra to share with future entrepreneurs?

My personal mantra is, "Lead with your life," and for me that means to lead authentically, lead vulnerably, and lead as you. There's really no other way.

Pamela Pekerman

FOUNDER, HUSTLE LIKE A MOM

We met in 2010, when you were in the trenches hosting events. How did you get to that point?

Not long before we were introduced, I'd closed my first company, BagTrends.com, which I'd launched during my senior year in college, in 2005, when online fashion content was not yet a thing. I remember thinking, *Let me just buy this little domain, and I'll have a working résumé when I graduate, so I can show editors how well I write. Then, naturally, I'll become the next Anna Wintour!*

So, I invested all of the money I'd acquired by the age of twenty-one, which amounted to $1,000 and seemed astronomical back then (it still seems like a lot). One thing led to another—it was a combination of right time, right place—and this thing that was supposed to pad my résumé ended up becoming my first business. I should say that I do also believe it has to be the right person. I'm a talker, a connector, and an ideas machine. That helped me grow Bag-Trends, as I was not only thinking for myself; I shared ideas and connections/potential partnerships with others. When you support others without an agenda, your network (quickly followed by your net worth) expands at a rapid pace. My network, including you and others in this book, is a result of being a giving tree. And my network is why I'm still hustling today, despite pivots, a pandemic, and plenty of personal pain.

Anyway, by the time I graduated, I had published what I considered my first magazine issue online. Fast-forward a few months and things began developing in the online space, which I was at the center of, creating this legit digital magazine called BagTrends.com. It started to get attention in the press, which led to guerrilla marketing on my part. I then hired a bunch of interns from New York University, where I'd gone to college, and went to my first New York Fashion Week. Within a year, I realized that I should turn BagTrends into a shop as well, and it ended up becoming the original contemporary handbags store online and a pioneer in the merging of e-commerce and editorial content within one destination.

Within two and a half years, we started hosting BagTrends "Arm Candy" parties, and suddenly I was throwing these amazing events, while running my online shop. The business was very successful, and I ended up doing a lot of television appearances for networks like VH1, where I would appear as their handbag expert and talk about the fabulous lives of celebrities and their accessories. I loved it, but one big mistake I made was allowing myself to get disconnected from the online space and that community I was building. Sure, hundreds of people were showing up to my events, but I was no longer in touch with the pulse of my brand. Additionally, around that time, my father passed away. And, within a year, this was around 2010, I abruptly closed BagTrends.

Do you have any regrets about shuttering BagTrends.com?

I don't regret closing it, because I think that everything happens for a reason. What I do regret is that it was so abrupt, and that I didn't respect the community I had built for so long. I was like, well, this isn't serving me anymore so I'm going to move on to something else. HSN [formerly Home Shopping Network] had been knocking on my door, and TJ Maxx was giving me an awesome contract, and I was ready for bigger things.

Now that I'm in my late thirties growing my current company, Hustle Like a Mom, I realize you can't do that. My community probably would have followed me, but instead I decided to start anew. It didn't have to be that way for me, and it shouldn't have been that way for them. Today, when I'm coaching mom entrepreneurs via Hustle Like a Mom, I always say drop the word *customer*, replace it with *community*, and the way you approach your business is going to be drastically different. That one mental shift empowers you to stay connected to your community and its emotional needs. It's not going to be about a grind, it's going to be a hand-holding situation. Your brand will have a genuine interest in the people versus in their wallets. And that's when you create magical loyalty that sustains you through even the hardest of times with your business. You start to care, and they start to trust and share your awesomeness with others.

Tell us about your current company, Hustle Like a Mom, and what the word *hustle* means to you.

Hustle Like a Mom is a multimedia platform and events brand that focuses on empowering and educating moms to build a successful bridge from mom life to entrepreneur life. Our events include informative panels, networking opportunities, and mompreneur brand showcasing. The mission of Hustle Like a Mom is to ensure every mom can live a life that allows her to align her personal and professional aspirations.

It's funny, we talk about this word *hustle*, and it's part of the name of my business, but I think sometimes it feels like a heavy word. What it means to me is that I'm connected to my needs. In other words, I have to put my ear to my heart and ask myself, what do I really need in this period of my life? And that represents a combination of personal, professional, financial, and emotional needs.

The other aspect of hustling, which—for me—has matured over time, is that I have to be realistic with my schedule. To succeed you need to operate, not only on the best-case days, but every day. It's so important to be honest with yourself about your own limitations.

Before I officially launched Hustle Like a Mom, my kids were young, and I was traveling the country. I had great contracts, and I was doing a lot of TV segments, everywhere from Miami to New York to Los Angeles. But I was still operating with the ambition I had in my twenties, even though I was in my mid-thirties, and those ambitions no longer served me. I felt like I was dragging around all of this old stuff that used to be great for me, but now it was holding me back. As a mom with little kids, I still wanted to be ambitious, and I still wanted a career. I just needed to find a new, more grown-up version of what it meant to hustle that would allow me to be the kind of mom I wanted to be.

This book is geared toward entrepreneurs of all ages. Looking back, did you find that it was hard to say "no" early on in your career?

Prior to having children, I thought they were going to easily incorporate into my life as it was. I figured I could keep doing all of my TV segments across the country and continue to say yes, yes, yes, to everything. Unfortunately, that was not realistic, at least not for me. Now when I say yes, I'm very focused and deliberate and committed to that yes. And I'm very happy saying no, because I think the more we know what we need, the easier it is for us to say no to the things that don't serve us. Obviously, in the beginning, you want to go out of your way to establish yourself and to be perceived as somebody who is a doer, a creator, and somebody that people can rely on, but at some point, you also have to be aware of the value of your time.

I believe that success comes in many forms, but with success, there can be frustration. Do you still experience this?

Yes! I definitely still get frustrated. I can't imagine anybody who doesn't. Entrepreneurship is creating something out of nothing. And many entrepreneurs—like the two of us—didn't have connections in our industries. We just had great ideas that we wanted to pursue through grit, ambition, desire, and commitment. It's not just about dreaming; it's about doing. So, absolutely, through all of that, there are a lot of frustrating moments. The way I've learned to combat my frustration is by going inward for a hot minute. There's an expression that says something like, "You can't see your reflection unless you stop and look at the water."

This is something that hit me hard and heavy, particularly during the pandemic, but I also believe that it's going to serve me and my community. The only difference between a pause and progress is judgment. I don't have time to judge myself, and if someone is judging me, I'm old enough to not give a damn.

At the moment, I'm consciously taking a six-week semi-pause. What does that mean? It means I pause certain things. It doesn't mean that I'm not nurturing my community, it doesn't mean that I'm not navigating my business, it just means that I'm not creating something new in that process. So, I think when you get frustrated and you are creating, creating, creating, you need to take a break. And that's okay.

Standing still is not being stagnant. Standing still takes strength, the strength to observe your business, assess if your personal and professional aspirations are aligning, and reflect on if what you are creating is truly serving the needs of your community.

The hustle matures. You evolve. Your community evolves. You must take time to ensure you're feeling your own heartbeat and that of your community. That's what a mature entrepreneur learns over time. That's a key lesson I hope to leave with all who engage with Hustle Like a Mom.

Nicole Purcell

CEO, CLIO AWARDS

We worked together on my first solo Fashion Week show, which was also your first show in Los Angeles. What encouraged you to approach me/BOY MEETS GIRL®?

I was the president of Rock Media at the time and one of our partners was *ELLE* magazine. I remember learning about you through them and then seeing your clothing. I thought you had such a cool brand, so when we were looking for designers for our Los Angeles show, I knew I had to meet you. Once that happened, I fell in love. Besides having a great product, I thought you were so genuine, and that lit my fire to want to work with you.

There were so many components to that show—everything from sponsorships, seating arrangements, and hiring models to hair and makeup, music, and actually getting the product there. What was it like creating that?

My background is events, and a fashion show is a huge production. For my company, it made sense to focus on amazing locations like Miami, Los Angeles, and New York and also brands that we thought had unique potential. Sometimes we did ten to fifteen shows a day, with the goal of helping designers gain more visibility. It was a tremendous amount of work, because there were so many pieces to the puzzle, but it was also very gratifying to collaborate with so many talented individuals.

I've had a few partners throughout my journey—some good, some not so good. Can you tell me more about your partnership at the time? Did it make you stronger?

Partnerships can be very tricky. I know this because my partner at Rock Media turned out to be a sociopath, which I did not know at first. It was mostly his company—he was funding it, and I came in after the fact. I will say that he was very good at sales and bringing on affiliates like *ELLE* magazine and Russell Simmons, but I ran all the business dealings with them. He would sell them a bill of goods, and then it was up to me to make the fashion events and everything else happen. Fortunately, I love growing companies, so that piece of it was fine. Unfortunately, he was stealing from our business account to finance his personal life, which was not fine. He would actually sit in front of me and say, "What do you mean? I didn't take anything," which I found out was a boldfaced lie. So, I had to walk away from the whole business because nothing was going to change. He kept embezzling, and we were in the hole for a lot of money.

Interestingly, this partnership did make me a lot stronger, though not in the way you might think. What it taught me, which is a very valuable lesson, is to be careful. I ended up investing my own money into that company and, as a result, my family almost lost everything. It definitely changed me as a person, as well as a businesswoman. I'm a better leader because of it. I'm not just going to listen to what somebody says or move forward without research and making sure the right people are around me.

How did you come to be the CEO of the Clio Awards?

After leaving Rock Media, I took a year off and then started looking for a job in New York. I sent my résumé in, like many other candidates, for an events/conference position at Prometheus Global Media, which owned *Hollywood Reporter, Billboard, Adweek*, and the

Clio Awards. As luck would have it, the vice president saw a little bit of herself in me and gave me the job. I learned so much in that position, working with publishers and editors, running events and conferences for all of the brands. From experience, I knew how to deal with all different types of people. I'd had bosses who would yell, I'd had a business partner who stole—so, I was able to roll with the punches.

About a year and a half later, the CEO of the company to whom I'd started reporting was reorganizing and asked if I wanted to work on the *Billboard* Music Awards with him. I said, "Well, you have a big team working on that already. Instead, I'd like the Clios, if I can have them."

He thought that I was crazy and replied, "It's an event once a year, Nicole, you're nuts."

And I said, "It's a brand. It makes money, has amazing clients from agencies and brands, and I want it."

So, he agreed, as long as I remained involved with other aspects of the company as well. That was eleven years ago, and it was the best career move for me.

Can you share a few words of wisdom for people trying to break into the world of event production?

I have everyone send their kids to me, so I've been talking to a lot of young women, specifically, to help them find internships and jobs. There are a few things that I believe are very important in this process. The first is having internships while you're in college. Not only will this provide you with experience, but it will also allow you to figure out what you like and don't like about an industry. Another thing is learning to deal with various kinds of people. This isn't easy and, often, people don't understand that if someone has a dissimilar personality to yours or does things in a way that you might not, that's not necessarily a bad thing. You have to try to work together harmoniously. You're never going to have a whole team that's wonderful, where everyone is exactly like you, and you don't want that either.

Communication is another huge thing. With technology today—phones, emails, and texts—you have to be able to keep in touch with your clients and your team. But I'm also a firm believer in meeting with people face-to-face and looking them in the eyes. I see a lot of kids today who are on their phones so much that, when you're talking to them or telling them a story, they're still focused on their device or they're drifting off. That's going to be a real challenge for them, especially after COVID, now that people are going back to the office. People need to be able to listen to their leaders and have conversations with them. It's a good thing to teach younger generations, because I'm not sure they're learning that in high school or college.

When you take the time to meet with someone, do you still expect a traditional thank-you note? Or is an email or text a suitable replacement?

I'm old school, so I appreciate when someone puts the effort in to write a traditional note. I still do, and I tell my team to do the same. It's easy to fire off a quick email after an interview, which is better than nothing, but I think it also shows that maybe you're not into the job.

You've been kind enough to invite me to the Clio Awards, and I'm always impressed by how personable you are with everyone who's there. As the CEO, how important is it to be that hands on?

Even though I don't own the Clio Awards, I run them, so in a sense, I feel like they're mine. And I teach my staff to treat the business like it's theirs as well. I'm still very hands on, though I do think that COVID changed things a little bit. Before COVID, I was involved with everything, and I really enjoyed it. It's important to show your team what you're doing and not just tell them what to do. But the pandemic definitely shifted my perspective. I was never a proponent of working from home. As I said, I believe in talking to people face-to-face. However, over the past year, I've been able to loosen the reins and not be on top of everyone all the time. I have a great team in place now. We've been through a lot together, and they are capable of running things, which is a nice feeling. It's one of my greatest pleasures to see my staff excel. I feel very fortunate with that, because it allows me to concentrate on the big picture and on new ideas.

Veronica Webb

MODEL, ACTRESS, WRITER, TV PERSONALITY

You've built a major personal brand over the years. How did you safeguard it? Did you hire an intellectual property lawyer to protect your name?

In my day, people didn't really talk about IP [intellectual property]. And, to be honest, I kind of missed the boat. I had VeronicaWebb.com for a long time and then it lapsed and someone has been squatting my name on the internet for the last twenty years or so. They're demanding the outrageous sum of $250,000 to buy it back. It's like if you own your house and a stranger moves in, and you can't kick them out.

It's your name/brand and, yet, you'd have to pay an exorbitant amount of money to get it back. How does that make you feel?

Of course it makes me angry—I have no idea how much business I've lost because of it, but I'm much more aware of protecting my brand now. Anytime a new media platform comes out—whether it's Instagram or Clubhouse or TikTok—I read about it and immediately go on and reserve my name.

You've worked with almost all of the top fashion designers throughout your career. Did you ever see their pieces get ripped off by other designers?

Yes, absolutely, but my role is not to act as a couture cop. It's to portray whatever product I'm engaged with and contractually paid to represent and to show it in the best light. You kind of have to separate yourself a little bit and let the public decide if it's a good product or not. There are certain things I won't attach my name to, like cigarettes, because they're detrimental to people's health. But I've never refused a garment unless there's something obscenely wrong with it. I've also had designers and stylists alike treat me as though I were being totally unreasonable when I've requested not to wear a completely see-through outfit on a runway or in a fashion shoot. I've had to cancel and that's gotten me canceled more than once from bookings. If you really have a problem with the clothing, your agent's job is to politely decline.

How did you break into the modeling scene?

I always wanted to be a model, and my mother said, "No." She grew up on a farm as did her mother and her mother's mother, and I grew up watching them make clothing—knitting, quilting, spinning yarn, dyeing shoes, and upholstering—those things were constantly happening in our house. For that reason, fashion has been part of my love language and my personal history forever; it represents empowerment, because for generations African Americans mostly did civil and military service—jobs that required wearing a uniform. So, in my family, fashion was a celebration and an expression to telegraph to the world where we came from and where we wanted to go in life. Regardless, a career in fashion, specifically as a model, was not something that my mother was excited about for me.

Now, being a mother with teenage girls, one of whom was thinking about modeling and did a couple of jobs with me, I can't believe the foresight that my mother had. Her feeling was, you don't need to make a living based on your looks before you have an education under your belt or the skills to create an alternative career. You need to know how to get by on your personality and your intellect. It was great that my mother said no to me for mental health reasons. It was also one of the best lessons I ever got in protecting my brand and protecting myself, which is that when you go into business, everyone you meet is going to say "no" to you until you figure out a way to prove yourself. Basically, as a model, anytime you go see a designer, a photographer, or a magazine editor, it's like you're going to the bank, and the bank has to approve you, because they're about to spend money with you as a business. My mother taught me how to turn a "no" into a "yes" from a very early age.

When I decided to pursue a career in fashion, I knew I had to get myself to New York, so I applied for a scholarship at the Parsons School of Design. That was step one of getting into the business. I didn't know if I would end up being a designer or an animator. Honestly, I didn't even give modeling much thought other than as an impossible dream. Then I got discovered while I was working as a cashier in SoHo.

I told my parents that I was going to try modeling and dedicate myself to it full-time. The first thing they said was: "Now you're starting a business, so the money we spent to help you go to college, which you're not finishing, should be considered a loan. You need to pay that back."

The next thing my mother said to me was: "You are now self-employed. You have no pension, no health insurance. When you get your first check, even if it's fifty dollars, put that money aside and start a 401(k)." She instilled in me that you have to save, because the only person you can ever really count on for the important things like your health and the roof over your head is you.

You were the first Black model to land a major cosmetic deal. How did that come about?

There are very few professions where women don't experience a glass ceiling, based on gender. And modeling is one of those professions.

Unfortunately, my sisters—one is a teacher and the other is a physician—had to fight dual obstacles of both race and gender. When I first started in the business, the generally accepted rule was that Black girls don't get covers, advertising, or cosmetic contracts.

Remember, I was born in 1965, which was the year that African Americans actually became full citizens in all fifty states, segregation was outlawed, and we were able to vote. So, when I was coming into my peak earning years as a model in the early nineties, there was still a lot of that. The assertion was that Black people would just buy anyway and therefore products didn't need to be made for us, and we didn't need to be marketed to. In line with that, the feeling in my industry was that Black models didn't have to be paid the same, because we were less valuable—which sends a message to the consumer that they aren't valuable either.

Thankfully, for me, the perfect confluence of events occurred. The entire socioeconomic demographic of the United States shifted to reflect a 1990 *Time* magazine cover story on "The Browning of America." In truth, most of fashion happens behind the velvet curtain. Due to the hard work and determination of African American cosmetic chemist and Revlon Account Executive Jerri Baccus-Glover, her dream of an affordable, mass-marketed cosmetics line for women of color was fully realized. She made makeup that any woman of color could get at any drugstore, which at the time was a major feat. It was called—if you can believe it—"Color Style."

Fortunately, the people at Revlon were open-minded and smart enough to make it happen and be the first ones to do it. They were thought leaders in the industry.

I come from a family of firsts—my mother was the first generation of commissioned officers in the U.S. Army. My sister is the first Black woman oncologist in the state of Michigan. My other sister is one of the first Black educators to write curriculums for Title One schools, which are underfunded, in order to bring kids up to grade level so they can graduate on time. And my aunt was the first Black nursing professor at Columbia. I felt a responsibility to open the door and pave the way. I'd be lying if I said it didn't go to my head a little bit at the time. But I also knew how important it was to make sure the opportunity remained for those who followed in my footsteps and to mentor other young women who didn't necessarily understand how to take those steps without someone showing them.

What advice would you give to new models starting out?

The first thing models who are just starting out should ask themselves is: *Am I doing the things that give me more personal strength?* Mental health comes first, physical comes second, and financial, third. You have to think about who you're choosing to spend time with, what kinds of conversations you're having, what you're eating, the way you're treating your body, and the way you're handling your money. If all of those things are taken care of, then your career stuff will fall into place. If you're doing something that's lessening your strength or not adding to your strength, you need to cut it, because it's not serving you, and it's probably serving someone else, most likely to your detriment.

Also, you have to keep your eyes on the prize and identify what you're working toward. If you're just out there every day, like, *Choose me, pick me, I want to be part of the fashion world,* then you don't really have much to anchor yourself to. But, if you say to yourself, *I want to buy an apartment, I want to go back to school,* or *I want to help my family,* those are very specific, concrete goals. Many young women don't realize that they should be telling their agents what their financial objectives are. They have to say, "I'd like to be earning this much money this year. How can we work together to make that happen?" Model your career after someone whom you admire.

Fashion's a business where women are physically competing against each other with a standard that's not empirical. It's not like basketball or gymnastics, where you either stick the landing or make the dunk or you don't. Half the time, you don't know why you get hired or why you don't. It could be your hair, your legs, your smile, your eye color, or your height in relation to everyone else whom they're booking. Modeling can make you extremely freaked out and paranoid about how you look. No matter how much you're working out, how strong you are, or how thin you are, you always feel like there's something wrong with you.

Another big reason why you really have to guard your mental health is that, as a model on set, you're the focus of everyone's problems. If the lighting or the hair or the makeup or the clothes aren't right, everyone is looking at and projecting it onto you as an object. It's hard not to take it personally. As a young person with inherent insecurities, it's especially difficult. Even now, sometimes I'll do a booking and, as much as I love my job, there's also part of me that can feel like shit, which is pretty remarkable since I've done about fifty thousand shoots in my career.

That's the dark side of being a model, but I wouldn't still be in this industry if I weren't more positive than negative, and if I weren't passionate about it. There's nothing like being in a room full of creative people of every race, color, preference, orientation, nationality, and creed, with amazing energy and ideas flowing toward creating a single goal. You learn so much and feel so good when the lights go up and everything happens. It's this great sense of camaraderie and accomplishment, and you're inspired.

The last piece of advice I'd give is to remember that everything you do represents you. Every meeting, every phone call, every email, and every text, starting from your first point of contact with your business. Always keep in mind that you're talking to a human being on the other side, and you're in the service industry. If I were teaching someone how to come into a business and how to make clients feel like they had an outstanding hire, I'd say: Ask them how they're doing, find out what they need, and tell them you're going to do your maximum to make it happen.

Christina Rice

CHIEF EXPERIENCE OFFICER, OMNOIRE

You've owned a few businesses. What have been some of the challenges along the way?

I've been an entrepreneur since I was twenty-one years old and that was twenty-two years ago. Over the past two decades, one of the biggest challenges has been finding and hiring good people. As the founder of companies, I've always looked for employees who can fill a gap for me, and it's taken me a really long time to learn to properly communicate exactly what that is. Every time I started a business, it was like being a new mother all over again. So, with each one I had to rediscover myself and understand how to train and groom my staff in a way that helped me move forward.

The real obstacle for me has been holding on to the great employees, because individuals in this generation don't stay in jobs for very long, rarely more than a year. They tend to hop around, which I actually encourage, since they have to figure out what their passions are as well. Another tricky aspect of being a boss, specifically an entrepreneur, is budgeting. There's always that little bit of fear attached to sustainability and growth and figuring out what our salaries will be—how much we can afford to pay people at different stages of the business. There are so many layers to being a founder.

What do you look for when you hire someone to join your team?

I look for people who are familiar with the wellness space so that they have some kind of basic understanding of what we do and our focus on community building. I also go off of someone's energy. Anyone who works for me has to appreciate our company values, which are integrity, transparency, wellness, and mindfulness. I groom my employees as interns over a short period of time before I actually bring them on as paid employees. Because what we do is centered around mental health, I have to make sure that the people who join my team are mentally and emotionally well so they can manage everything we do internally and with our community too.

Have you ever had to fire anyone and how did it make you feel?

When I worked in public relations, I had to fire a woman on the spot who worked for me at one of the New York Fashion Week shows we did. She'd just made too many major mistakes. Any time you have to let someone go who's been an intricate part of your team, it feels like a great loss. I always experience a little bit of a pain, but when your business is your baby, you have to do what's best for you and your future. I think it's different when you have hundreds of people who work for you. As someone who runs smaller, more intimate companies, I have close connections with my employees, so it's definitely hard. With that said, as a leader, you have to remember that the people who work for you are watching what you do, and sometimes you have to make a split-second decision, no matter how agonizing it may be.

As a woman leader and entrepreneur, are your emotions part of your decision-making process or can you separate the two completely?

I separate them completely. I go with my gut instinct and leave my emotions out of it. I ask myself what feels right to me in any given moment and try not to let fear, insecurity, or anxiety get in the way. Then I make the decision whether to do it or not. I've learned that I have a very defined center and that I can trust myself to know what's right.

When we did our first New York Fashion Week show together, things got a little wonky. How did you stay in control and manage your team?

I still have PTSD from that event! I remember how hard we'd worked leading up to that fashion show. I think we were awake until about 4:00 a.m. most nights and then would hit the ground running at 7:00 a.m. We had a system in place and were prepared for the show to run very smoothly, and then it all blew up. I was having my own internal meltdown, but I also knew that I had to be there for my team. One thing I instill in everybody I work with is that there's always a solution. You have to take a breath and a moment and then get on with it. Nothing ever goes perfectly, so you need to have a treasure chest of quick fixes at all times, whether it's a custom service issue, a tech breakdown, or simply dealing with individuals who are having their own meltdowns. You have to put your emotions aside, strategize, and focus. In the end, we put on a great show, in large part thanks to you!

What's one key thing that you've learned from your various businesses that serves you today?

At twenty-one, I was the first Black woman founder and owner of a high-end, luxury boutique in Nashville, Tennessee, which I ran for more than four years before I burned out and started to question whether Nashville was the place for me. Ultimately, I closed the boutique, sold all of the merchandise, and moved to New York to begin a career in public relations. I worked at a few different PR companies for another four years, and then in 2010, I got laid off from my job and decided to launch my own PR agency. I had my agency from 2010 to 2018, but around 2015 I was already looking for something new. I'd lost my passion for PR, and I started taking yoga and embarking on an extensive spiritual journey.

That's when I came up with the idea for my current company, OMNoire, which is a health and wellness platform for women of color. So, from 2016 to 2018, I started the transition out of PR, and I shut down my agency in 2018 to focus on OMNoire full-time. That's been my career ever since. While it may seem like I have "entrepreneur ADD," I prefer to view it as "founder fluidity." The main thing that I've learned is to know when it's over for me and when it's time to move on. That's been my journey—I start a business, see it through, and when I'm no longer happy or fulfilled in that career, I pursue something else that excites me.

Rosario Dawson

ACTRESS, PRODUCER, AND ACTIVIST

You started acting at a young age. How did that come about?

I grew up on the Lower East Side of New York, and one day my dad told me to go downstairs and get discovered because there was a Vibe commercial shooting on the block, so I hung out on our stoop for a few days. I got cast in the commercial, and I was there when Larry Clark and Harmony Korine were walking by with their director of photography and other crew members scouting locations for the film *Kids*. They asked if I would audition, and I got the part. When the film came out, I decided to continue pursuing acting with the support of my friends and family. My grandmother paid for me to go to The Lee Strasberg Theatre & Film Institute for one semester, where I met my friend Talia Lugacy, when she was fifteen and I was sixteen.

All these years later, our film, *This Is Not a War Story*, that we produced and that she wrote, directed, and starred in, which was our dream when we were teenagers, just got picked up by HBO Max. It's so amazing that chance moments like sitting on my stoop as a child, hoping to be cast in a commercial, can turn into intention, conviction, and commitment. It's been really beautiful exploring what was discovered that day, which was not me by the industry, but rather the industry by me.

I know your mother very well, and she's super fierce. Did she inspire you with the confidence she possesses to become who you are today?

I come from a long line of women—we're "the Isabels." I'm Rosario Isabel, my mom is Isabel Celeste, my grandmother is Isabel, and my great-gran was Celestina; that's where the Celeste comes back again. I've always been very particular about us Isabels and the coven that we are together—just the magic that is us, knowing each other and loving each other in this life. The sacrifices that were made and built upon, along with the dignity and tenacity with which they were enacted, have always been my biggest inspiration.

Have you ever felt completely satisfied on your journey, or do you have an entrepreneurial spirit that always pushes you to want to do more?

I definitely would say I have an entrepreneurial spirit. I believe that curiosity, kindness, excitement, empathy, compassion, and love can exist in creativity. That's been my experience in so many different arenas and spaces, from organizational work to film and acting work to time and energy invested in family. All of my values and the things that I care about are part of everything I do.

There used to be this pressure to pick a cause, pick a direction, or pick a genre, which doesn't exist as much now. I feel like we've really shifted gears into perceiving that we're multidimensional people and there's intersectionality and interdependence. I think the pandemic and quarantine period made people ponder quite a lot of things. My conclusion is that what we devote time to should be a reflection of who we are, what we want to create, and what we want to leave behind in this world. For me, it's been really exciting to say yes to so many things that motivate me artistically.

You introduced me to the Lower Eastside Girls Club about a decade ago. What drew you to work so closely with them?

As I mentioned, I grew up on the Lower East Side of Manhattan. It was a tough time, because we were living in one of the many abandoned buildings there. People often romanticize the eighties and nineties, but not everybody came out of it alive. It was pretty intense, but it was also really magical. There were beautiful gardens that people like Bette Midler fought to maintain. It's a real community there, and I feel connected to it, which I don't necessarily feel in other places in the world.

Living there as a child, I witnessed poor people helping poor people, really standing up for each other, and not expecting anyone else to come and do it for them. I remember being very engaged, very present, and very alive. That tenacity always spoke to me. My parents had the imagination and the fortitude to believe they could raise a family there, someplace where I walked to a good school.

It was a very artistic and wild sort of upbringing in my particular neighborhood, and the people who run the Lower Eastside Girls Club encapsulate, remind, record, and archive the greatness and the funkiness of the Lower East Side and all of its quirks and bells and whistles. It's just such a special place with its thirty thousand square feet of awesomeness. There are so many resources; they're truly going above and beyond. Nothing is out of bounds, which has always been their way and it really speaks to my spirit. It's also a totally free program, which you can't beat. To think that I was that misfit little girl on the Lower East Side and didn't have a space like that to go to and now it exists, is just magnificent to me. I love sharing it with people. It really is my heart.

You've been an amazing supporter of mine, attending my shows, and wearing my brand. What was it like to form Studio One Eighty Nine with Abrima Erwiah, and where do you see it in the next five years?

Studio One Eighty Nine is an artisan-produced, fashion, lifestyle brand and social enterprise that's made in Africa and produces African and African-inspired content and clothing. Like you, my partner, Abrima, is so supportive, clear, dynamic, brilliant, and talented. I loved your question about the Lower Eastside Girls Club, because you've been so incredible with them, and that's how you are with everyone you touch. That's so much of what we want to be at Studio One Eighty Nine—two friends who love each other, are inspired by each other, and want to be there for each other.

Through that we've become businesswomen, and we've got these incredible companies and organizations that we collaborate with regularly (Warby Parker, OkayAfrica, EDUN, CFDA [Council of Fashion Designers of America]). It's blood, sweat, and tears, but we've been very lucid about our intention, which is fashion as an agent of social change. We strive to recognize people along the entire supply chain and evolve the fashion industry to be more regenerative, sustainable, authentic, and empathetic. We want to see the individuals behind and in front of the camera, the clothing, the process, and the buying and the selling. Where does this stuff go? Who makes your clothes? It's a major shift within an industry that is the second largest polluter on the planet.

It's so necessary when we talk about climate change, and people don't necessarily see that correlation, but it's imperative that they do. It's been really powerful to be able to champion that and to see just how much Studio One Eighty Nine has grown. It's the turning of the whole conversation everywhere, a change in consciousness that's happening. It's extraordinary to imagine where Studio One Eighty Nine could be in five years. I know we'll be ready for whatever comes, because we're building it organically.

Cassandra Bankson

SKINCARE EXPERT, MEDICAL AESTHETICIAN, AND
YOUTUBE CREATOR

Please share the story of how I discovered you and what it was like to walk in your first New York Fashion Week show.

Nine years ago, I was represented by a modeling agency, and I remember BOY MEETS GIRL® being interested in a casting video I had submitted. I was super nervous about my acne and recall getting ready three times before I finally found the courage to film a runway walk outside by my parents' pool in the backyard. I honestly didn't think that I would get picked, because I was used to my acne preventing me from booking jobs in the past. But not only did you see something interesting about the way I walked, you saw that there was something different about how I carried myself—literally and metaphorically. You booked me for the fashion show, but more important, you believed in me.

Behind the scenes at New York Fashion Week, the makeup artist told me to remove all of my foundation and go barefaced so he could create the same look the other models had. Even with my severe acne, he worked with me, and he didn't make me feel insecure or overly ugly at any point. You made a point to share with the media that you were casting different models for your show, including me, because of the beauty and individuality you saw in each of us. That to me was not only a wonderful work opportunity, but something that truly helped me build my self-confidence at a pivotal time in my life.

How did that experience make you feel?

Being cast and being able to walk in that show made me feel both nervous and confident. I remember shaking my shoulders and letting the excitement run through my toes a bit that day, moments before I stepped onto the runway. Being chosen by someone to represent their brand, while they were fully aware that I had flaws, was reassuring. You saw the human side of me and accepted me for who I was, and that was reflected in what your clothing line stood for. You weren't trying to modify me or make me somebody else. It was one of the unspoken ways that I felt truly seen and accepted.

In what ways did it build your confidence?

At the beginning of this journey, my confidence was in question. Imposter syndrome is real, and there have been so many times in my modeling career that I felt like I was "faking it" and someone was going to "figure me out." When were they going to see me without my makeup? Will they judge me for my acne? Because I had started sharing my YouTube videos online with my bare skin, would they dislike me and rip away an opportunity that I so desperately needed the income to live off of?

On the day of the first show, I was "in denial nervous." It was a surreal moment when somebody saw the real me and didn't hate it, and I don't think I was able to fully absorb or process that moment until months later. Walking on the runway was like walking on a cloud—it didn't feel real and almost like a fever dream. I floated along the runway and the flashes were more like suggestions than things that demanded my attention. It didn't sink in that I was living the dream until the days and weeks after.

I took off the shield and the veil that had been constricting me to the point that I couldn't be my authentic self. Walking in your show was one of the first pivotal moments of me being able to, not only step onto the runway, but step into who I truly am, rather than who someone else wants me to be.

Did those first steps lead to where you are today?

Yes! When I started out as a model, I was hiding behind makeup, distraught over my acne and my body, in an abusive relationship, and spending time with friends and people who didn't respect me. I was not in a good place, and you loved and embraced me for who I was, and not for a façade I was trying to put on.

You weren't just a designer I was working with; you became a friend and a mentor. You helped me see what was possible out of life. It took another year or two, but I ended up getting out of that controlling relationship. I ended up becoming more confident going to the grocery store without my makeup. I was able to go to the pool in the summer without a shawl over my acne-ridden shoulders for the first time in almost eight years. When a casting agent turned me down because of my skin, it no longer meant that I was going to stay in my room and cry for the rest of the day. And it's because of those experiences on the runway with you that I realized fashion is not about perfection, it's an expression of humanity. And perfection does not exist—we contribute to this world not by fitting a specific standard, but by expressing what we each do uniquely.

Today, as the acne big sister of the internet, I recognize that you inspired me to share my vulnerability with others time and time again through my content and the growth of my own business. I've also been able to mentor other young girls and artists who have struggled with their skin and, thanks to you, I approach them with a similar care and attention to sensitivity that you showed me. For that, I will be forever grateful.

Katya Libin

COFOUNDER, HEYMAMA

What was your career before you started HeyMama, and what prompted the change?

Before I started HeyMama, I was the global director of sponsorships at Social Media Week, which was a conference that looked at the intersection of social media, technology, and innovation. That was actually my first experience with community building and doing real life events. It inspired me to start HeyMama in 2014, with my cofounder, when my daughter was around three years old. I just felt like there wasn't a community for working mothers that focused on bringing women together to help them figure out how to juggle a career and a family. And I wanted to create a community that celebrated mothers like me who were in this new stage of life that was incredibly overwhelming and scary.

HeyMama was really born out of that pain point and this overall feeling of isolation and not having a playbook on how to do it all. I knew I had to find other moms to help me get through that journey, and that if I could connect with these other women, the journey itself would be incredibly rewarding and way more fun than doing it all alone.

You're a single, working mom, and you make it look so easy, which I'm sure it's not. How do you balance your personal and professional lives?

For me, being a single mom has had its ups and downs. On the negative side, I miss my daughter so much when we're not together. I'm sure any single mom can relate to that feeling. On the positive side, when I don't have her, which is about 35 percent of the time, I do have the ability to work a bit later. So, the way that I handle it is, when I'm with my daughter, I try to stop working earlier. I take more breaks throughout the day, I pick her up from school, and we cook dinner together. It's important for me to be present with her, because she's ten now and needs me more than ever.

When I'm not with her, I invest more time in my professional life. It doesn't necessarily mean that I have balance every day. I aim for it more on a week-by-week basis. Some weeks are a little more chaotic, and I'll say to myself, *You're going to work your ass off for four days, and then you're going to recuperate for three days.* That ebb and flow, week by week, has proved to be effective for me. I can put my head down and get the job done when I need to, and then I can really show up as a mom when I need to.

How did your past experiences prepare you to pivot during the pandemic, and what did that look like?

The pivot for HeyMama was massive. We were doing about 180 events across twelve cities pre-COVID. Such a large part of our community was connecting in real life, and it was a very integral part of how we showed up in our members' lives. Then the pandemic hit. People were isolated in their homes and scared, because there was so much information to decipher. It was a whole new world, and it really bonded us as a community, because everyone was craving that connection. We leaned in hard on building a digital community and started bringing women together through digital events and digital programming. Basically, we were able to do a sharp right by taking the typical, real life experience and bringing it online for our members. A bonus was that it also allowed us to accept members from all around the country. So, our company ended up growing significantly during COVID, because the need for a digital community for working moms was strong, and we were doing it right, day in and day out. We wanted to provide as much support and value as we could for moms who were really struggling. Thankfully, our team is very nimble, super smart, and they work fast, which meant we were able to adjust to our new world.

What advice would you give to your younger self on being an entrepreneur?

The advice I would give myself is pretty similar to the advice I give now, which is: you have to possess the confidence to believe in yourself and take a huge leap of faith as far as what's coming down the line. I'd also tell my younger self, specifically when I started Hey-Mama, to move a bit slower. I know that sounds counterproductive when you're thinking about growing a business, but I believe it's better not to rush to get to a specific point.

Claudine DeSola

FOUNDER, CARAVAN

We met more than fifteen years ago, when you were running your company, THINK Public Relations. What attracted you to the world of public relations and marketing? And how has your job changed over the last two decades?

I always knew I wanted to get into public relations and creating experiences, events, pop-ups, and overall out-of-the-box ways to attract press. When I graduated from college, I was super lucky to land my first job doing marketing, PR, and events for the fashion designer YEOHLEE in New York. It was the era of the big Bryant Park fashion shows with all of the supermodels, so that experience was fantastic. After a few years doing that, I wanted to be able to work with different brands, so I took jobs at a few boutique agencies before starting THINK. It was important for me to choose the types of projects I engaged in, because, for example—like you—philanthropy is a significant piece of what I do. I love being in a position to help spread awareness about things like the environment and organizations such as the Humane Society. I believe it's essential to be proud and passionate about what you do.

The world of PR has obviously changed through the years. Traditional press is much more of a challenge. Magazines used to be thicker; it was a simpler equation. Now there are all of these new means of publicity—blogs, podcasts, and social networks like Clubhouse. Whereas PR used to be easily defined, these days there are a million outlets to think about. Career-wise, I've tried to evolve and learn as much as I can in these other aspects of PR, in order to create the content studio we have now. Storytelling for brands is key.

In 2005, while you were working at THINK, you also started Caravan, which was an RV, a recreational vehicle, that people could shop in, but the concept has changed over the years. Can you tell us about that?

Caravan has had a few renditions through the years. As with any industry, morphing, figuring out, and being patient is crucial. So, what began as an RV concept, and really a side project, is currently called Caravan Social Club. Throughout the pandemic, we showcased virtual programs and hope to return to in-person events very soon. I will say that the original experiment, which was to see if people would go shopping inside a Caravan, was very cool, as you know, because we sold BOY MEETS GIRL®! And it was also successful, but I was really terrible at figuring out the sell-throughs and math, and hiring tons of sales staff. I ended up taking the best parts of what I learned from Caravan and from THINK PR and combining them into the incarnation that's currently Caravan Social Club.

While I was struggling to get pregnant, you sent me a very helpful book called *Baby Steps: Having the Child I Always Wanted (Just Not as I Expected)* by the actress Elisabeth Röhm, who was going through in vitro fertilization. Can you share more about your journey of having your son, Tatum?

I was styling Elisabeth for TV appearances while she was doing her book tour, so that was how I found out about it and had the chance to speak to her about her path to getting pregnant. My own biological clock was ticking, and once I met my husband, Scott, at thirty-seven and we fell in love, I realized that I was later to the game than I'd even thought. I ended up jumping around from one doctor to another, which I've heard is common, but wasn't something I'd expected.

At one point, I did get pregnant from intrauterine insemination, but it turned out to be an ectopic pregnancy, which is when a fertilized egg is growing outside the uterus. The fetus was eight weeks old, but it wasn't a viable pregnancy, so I had to have surgery. I went through a lot with that because you have to have a tube removed, which makes it even harder to get pregnant. I also found out that I had two forms of blood-clotting disorder, which meant if I did get pregnant I would have to take additional medicine to keep the pregnancy safe. I always like to share that because a lot of women don't get tested for blood-clotting disorder, and it is something that can really affect a pregnancy.

As you know, even though there can be these kinds of hurdles, you have to keep going. And you have to say to yourself, *I want this to happen, my husband wants this to happen, we're going to do this.* It's all about finding the right perspective and the right doctors. It took us more than five years to get pregnant. The luckiest days were when we finally heard the good news, and when I was able to give birth to Tatum. I definitely did not take any of it for granted.

Honestly, it's like a job for some women to get pregnant. You have to research, read, go to panels, and interview doctors. Also, you're constantly finding out new information about your own body and trying new things; it's a lot of hours to put in. It absolutely affected my work and it impacted me hormonally. There were a lot of ups and downs, especially with all of the medicine I had to take. I give anyone who has or still is enduring it so much credit and support. People who haven't gone through it don't realize what a feat it is.

Since it took so long to have Tatum, did you want to take time off from work when he was born or were you determined to find a way to balance both?

I have to admit that I was on a project right before I gave birth, and I had a C-section, so I wound up staying in the hospital for longer than I'd expected. I was back on my laptop the day after having Tatum. I did my best to take a maternity leave and spend as much time with him as possible, but there were hours that I had to allocate to my work. There was never a total stopping point.

Now it's all about balance. Tatum goes to preschool and camp on weekdays, and I'm lucky that my mom lives with us and can help. I love that he can experience time with his grandma. But, there's also my career, cooking, cleaning, and being a wife—the plight of working moms everywhere. The pandemic was especially challenging because it was difficult to find activities to keep Tatum entertained and, in the beginning, he wasn't in preschool yet. I tend to take on the lion's share of parenting responsibilities since my husband's schedule is less flexible.

Do you think your persistence and work ethic kept you moving through-out everything?

I'm a type A personality, which probably helped a lot. It's in my genes. My mom is very persistent with everything she does, and my dad was the hardest worker I've ever known. He used to put in double shifts to pay for college for both of my brothers and private school for me. He would literally sleep a few hours and go right back to work, so he could afford everything. That perseverance was ingrained in me early on.

A lot of people go through hardship, some more than others, and I've definitely had a lot of "Are you kidding me?" moments in my life, but I always knew I had to keep going. I had tunnel vision. If I didn't, I would be in a much darker, different place in my life.

As far as getting pregnant, I was very fortunate to have a support team of great friends and family. Many women struggle with open-ing up about it and leaning on those around them. For me, it was things like seeing you have Dylan that kept me going. I said to myself, *If Stacy can do it, I can do it. Dylan needs to meet my future kid one day!*

Sixteen years after you launched the Caravan RV, you're bringing it back. What's it like to have this full-circle moment and be able to take your son on the road with you?

It's very exciting! Tatum is definitely doing some of the tour with us. One of my brothers lives out in California and the other is in Arkansas now, so it's a perfect opportunity to visit them. Life is a journey. And I think it's a beautiful thing to have your child see you work, even at the youngest age.

Sarah Andelman

FOUNDER AND FORMER CREATIVE DIRECTOR, COLETTE

How did you and your mom decide to start colette together? Were you both in the fashion business prior?

My mum was always a merchant, and I was just finishing my history of art studies at École du Louvre, back in 1996–1997. First, we fell in love with the location itself, when we moved into the building. Then we decided to bring together everything we were passionate about—from art and fashion to design, beauty, music, food, and more.

When you opened colette in 1997, you were ahead of the curve in changing the window displays every single week. What was the concept behind this?

We always considered the shop to be like a magazine, so the weekly change of the windows was like featuring new covers. We also rearranged the displays inside the store. It would be the same products, but introduced in a fresh way.

I had the honor of working with you on a few collaborations, and your teams were always very loyal and customer service oriented. How did you achieve that level of commitment from your employees?

By being present and trying to keep the team motivated, excited, and inspired.

In your twenty years owning colette, what did it mean to you to discover and work with a new brand?

I always loved discovering new brands with an innovative sense of creativity. And with the many collaborations we did, it was important to us to keep them organic.

You decided to close colette after two decades of great success, and your website read, "All good things must come to an end." How did it feel to have that incredible final party with lines down the street and so many customers, celebrities, and famous musicians there to celebrate?

We felt very grateful.

Michelle Park

COHOST, #MOMSGOTTHIS, JOURNALIST, TV HOST, AND
LIFESTYLE EXPERT

**Did you always want to be in front of the camera? What was your road
like to get there?**

No, I didn't always want to be in front of the camera. I went to
Stanford University and was prelaw. Then I met Juju Chang on
campus—she's also a Stanford grad and Korean American. Juju was
on ABC's *20/20* at the time, and I watched the show every Friday
night. She happened to be speaking on campus, and when I got to
meet her, she said, "I'll help you get a job at ABC." I couldn't believe
it. I had an offer to be a paralegal at a law firm, but, instead, I went
to work at ABC News with Juju.

I wanted to be an investigative producer, to tell people's stories,
especially those who had been historically voiceless or largely
ignored. I thought the best way to do that would be behind the camera, so I could have more autonomy and more control. Then I got an
offer from KNBC and moved to Los Angeles to work in their investigative unit, which was great. But, while I was there, my mentor
suggested that, as a Korean American woman, being on camera
would make a real difference. I just didn't think I had the type of
personality to be on camera. But it was that conversation that changed
the way I looked at it. If I was trying to give a voice to the voiceless
and to my community, especially Asian American women, who were
not being seen as three-dimensional people, the only way for me to
alter that perception was to be an Asian American woman on camera.

I definitely think I got lucky, which is a big part of getting on air. Of course there were moments during my career where I felt discouraged, like when I first started and had a boss who said I wasn't bubbly enough and told me I'd never make it on camera. Thankfully I also came in contact with so many people who said, "You can do this." My skill is interviewing. Usually within thirty minutes of talking to someone, I can get to know them to a point where they are willing to share something really interesting or deep.

We cocreated and cohosted a podcast called #MOMSGOTTHIS, featuring interviews with accomplished, inspiring entrepreneurs and entertainers who are also moms. Did you want to have children right away or did career come first? And did you struggle to find balance between the two?

I always knew I wanted to be a mom. I just had no idea how much labor and time it would entail, so I didn't wait to find a moment when I had a break in my career. Before I had my first daughter, I thought I would go right back to what I was doing after she was born. I was on the road constantly doing ground media tours across the country. I was also contributing to *The Steve Harvey Show* regularly in Chicago. You can't be a mom of an infant and do all that, which I didn't realize at first. I ended up putting my career on hold after I had my first baby. It was somewhat of a surprise how important it was for me to be with my baby during those initial six months. I loved that stage, which not every mom does. It was a moment of reckoning for me where I decided that I wasn't going to be at a network hosting a national show. If you want to do that, you need to be willing to work all the time, which I wasn't. I accepted that my career path was going to change, and I was going to continue to do what I loved, but not in the capacity that I'd been doing before.

How did our podcast inspire your motherhood journey?

The greatest thing about our podcast was talking to so many other moms. Motherhood is such a great equalizer. It doesn't matter if you're a billionaire, the CEO of a company, or whatever else. All of us have these tiny human beings to shape, and we're all starting from square one again. To be able to see that through the lens of our podcast and hear the thoughts, struggles, and wisdom from other moms was amazing. It filled my cup in the sense that I needed to discuss what I was going through with other women who were experiencing the same thing.

Are there aspects of motherhood that have shaped who you've become professionally and, in the reverse, has your job shaped who you are as a mother?

Since having children, I'm a different person with a different and stronger viewpoint when I tell a story. Early in my career, if someone asked me to do something, I typically did it. Now, I choose my stories carefully. As a mom of two young Korean American girls, I don't want to be putting content out there that's going to set back any race, gender, or sexual orientation, so I'm extremely thoughtful about it. I also think that being a journalist has shaped the way I mother because I approach life with an investigative journalism style. I read everything there is to read about parenting, and I listen to all of the angles. I want to hear from the mom who says time-outs are good, and I also want to hear from the mom who says time-outs are not okay. Also, when I speak to my kids about anything, I like to dig really deep, which is definitely a result of my professional background.

What advice would you give to working-moms-to-be?

I have so much advice for working-moms-to-be, but I believe the biggest thing is to remember to go easy on yourself and not to fall into the mind space where you think, *I'm not good at my job, I'm not good at raising my kids, and I'm not being a good wife.* You have to be gentle with yourself, because there will be days when two things win and one doesn't. Nobody's perfect. What you see on social media is not true. We're all struggling through it.

Sarah Clagett

TELEVISION PRODUCER, NBC *TODAY* SHOW

Did you always know you wanted to be a TV producer? What was that path like?

Not at all. It was kind of a crazy ride. I went to the University of Kansas and dated a guy from Chicago who'd been to New York City. He told me all about it, and I remember thinking, *Wow, that sounds amazing.* We then found out that the local radio station was giving away a trip to New York and, if you wanted to win, you had to go [to the station] in person. So, my boyfriend and I went down to the station and submitted our names and, sure enough, they picked me, which was completely unexpected, but also awesome!

Two days later, we boarded a plane for an adventure that I had no idea would change the trajectory of my life. Part of the prize was a tour of NBC, where we visited Conan O'Brien's show, and I absolutely loved it. It was my first time at a television station, and it definitely sparked my interest. I'd thought about TV production, but was undecided about what I really wanted to pursue, so that experience kind of pushed me in that direction. I went back to school five days later and said to myself, *How can I make that my life?* And I did. I worked very hard and, miraculously, all the stars aligned. By the grace of God, I managed to get an internship at NBC.

When my internship was ending, MSNBC—the twenty-four-hour news channel—was launching, and I applied for a job as a production assistant. I spent a year and a half on the network desk, and then from there I got a job as a researcher at the *Today* show in 2000. I've been there ever since.

When the pandemic hit, your family temporarily moved to Iowa. What was the impetus behind that decision? And did you feel that, despite the awful circumstances, you were where you were meant to be?

My dad lives in Iowa, and we visit him every year for the Fourth of July. In 2020, we weren't able to do that because of the pandemic so we waited until the end of the summer. At the time it had been a solid six months of my kids virtually learning, which was truly challenging for both me and my husband career-wise, family-wise, and relationship-wise. One evening, we were sitting having a glass of wine, figuring out what life was going to look like for us come fall. In-person school kept getting pushed back, and I started to panic. I love my job, but my family is clearly my priority, and the idea of enrolling my kids in school full-time in Iowa sounded amazing. The next day I took a tour of a small Catholic school there, which had fifty students from preschool to sixth grade. I figured because there were so few kids that the chance of them contracting COVID would be much lower. So, we decided to move there temporarily, and it was great for us. My husband and I were both able to work from home successfully, and our kids were supportive in all the ways we needed them to be. It was just a tremendous comfort that my kids were in a place that felt right for us and for them. Being in Iowa really slowed us down in the best way possible. It forced me to take stock of my life and allowed me to reconnect with my family, which was a blessing.

In your twenty-one years at the *Today* show, was this your first time producing segments remotely? How did you make this pivot look so effortless?

I'm glad you think I made it look effortless! And, yes, it was the first time I've truly produced segments virtually. I've traveled the world with correspondents for everything from hurricanes to school shootings, and of course happier stories too. But I would always field produce and send the footage back to New York where they would piece it together for me. For us to put our show on the air virtually day after day for a year and a half was wild and certainly rocky in the beginning. We did all of our segments on FaceTime or Skype, and sometimes the Wi-Fi didn't work. Our guests didn't know how to be their own cameramen, their own audio people, or their own set designers, and they had to do it all. It took a lot of coaching by the producers. My job quickly pivoted from being responsible for just the content to helping people figure out every aspect of what to do. It was hard, and we're still doing it. I'm hopeful that, slowly but surely, things will return to normal.

My son, Dylan, and your son Wyatt are good friends, and two years ago you shared your story on today.com that Wyatt spent 117 days in the NICU when he was born. Did that struggle help you cope when some of your family members got COVID?

My dad, my stepmom, and my husband all got COVID, but my boys and I didn't, which was a miracle. We literally holed up in this storage room in the basement of my dad's house in order to keep our distance. Wyatt is seven now and doing well, but he had a tough start to his life, so I still have some PTSD from that. It wasn't just those 117 days—I've worried about him getting sick all his life. Knowing that I've been able to push through that definitely prepared me for a global pandemic. I knew that if I could endure my son almost dying and all of the uncertainty as to whether he'd survive, I was strong. Even though that experience was hellish, it helped me become a better parent, and it helped Wyatt—which means "brave warrior"—become just that.

Do you feel like you're where you need to be now?

I do feel like I'm where I need to be and also where I should be, and where I want to be. Never in my wildest dreams did I think we would spend a year living in Iowa. My parents divorced when I was four, and since then I'd only spent maybe a week at a time living with my father, not 365 days. The global pandemic allowed me to get to know him so much better and, also—as cliché as it may sound—to stop and smell the roses. I actually wrote an article for a local Iowa newspaper on how nice everyone is there and about all the kind things that people did for me that blew me away, from filling my tank with gas when I thought I was going to run out, to giving my kids soccer cleats because I'd forgotten them. It made me realize that there are good people everywhere—you just have to find them.

Iowa was where I needed to be during that time, and New York is where I'm supposed to be now. I love my job. I want to be in the studio. I want my kids to go to the great schools here, and for my husband to continue his career. The last few years have been a journey, and that journey will continue. I'm always working toward something. I just might not know what it is at this moment.

INDEX

ABOUT THE AUTHOR

STACY IGEL is the founder and creative director of BOY MEETS GIRL®, a global impact brand known for its iconic double-silhouette logo and purposeful, edgy, contemporary athleisure wear. Stacy and BOY MEETS GIRL® seek to promote the message that confidence and courage are trends that never go out of style.

Stacy has had exclusive fashion partnerships with Paris's colette, Bergdorf Goodman, Roots Canada, Saks Fifth Avenue, Target, and NBA's Chicago Bulls and Atlanta Hawks, to name just a few. She collaborates with musical artists, athletes, and activists making an impact, as well as organizations including the Young Survival Coalition, BullyBust, Human Rights Watch, GLAM4GOOD, Youth Over Guns, and many others.

In 2016, Stacy's alma mater, the University of Wisconsin, awarded her with the Wisconsin Idea Alumni Award, which recognized Stacy for how she educated and influenced people's lives beyond the boundaries of a classroom. In 2017, Stacy won the "Forward Under 40" award, where the university acknowledged Stacy as one of the rising stars in her field for her achievement and positive impact on her community.

Stacy and BOY MEETS GIRL® have been featured in *InStyle, Elle, Cosmopolitan, Marie Claire, Allure*, PEOPLE, *Teen Vogue, Seventeen, Women's Wear Daily*, the *Wall Street Journal*, the *New York Times*, and dozens more. She is the cocreator and cohost of the podcast

#MOMSGOTTHIS, which was featured on Forbes as a "women-created podcast everyone should be listening to right now" and in less than a year ranked in the top 25 on iTunes. Stacy is a frequent lecturer and panelist on subjects like social media, philanthropy, branding, and entrepreneurship. She lives in New York City with her husband, Brian, and their son, Dylan.